Mind Builders

Mind Builders

Multidisciplinary Challenges for Cooperative Team-building and Competition

Paul Fleisher and Donald M. Ziegler

Teacher Ideas Press, an imprint of Libraries Unlimited
Westport, Connecticut • London

Library of Congress Cataloging-in-Publication Data

Fleisher, Paul.
    Mind builders : multidisciplinary challenges for cooperative team-building and competition /
by Paul Fleisher and Donald M. Ziegler.
      p. cm.
    Includes bibliographical references and index.
    ISBN 1-59158-376-4 (pbk. : alk. paper)
    1. Gifted children—Education—Handbooks, manuals, etc. 2. Student activities—Handbooks,
manuals, etc. 3. Problem-based learning—Handbooks, manuals, etc. 4. School contests. I. Ziegler,
Donald M. II. Title.
    LC3993.2.F58 2006
    371.95'6—dc22   2006023744

British Library Cataloguing in Publication Data is available.

Library of Congress Catalog Card Number: 2006023744
ISBN: 1-59158-376-4

First published in 2006

Libraries Unlimited/Teacher Ideas Press, 88 Post Road West, Westport, CT 06881
A Member of the Greenwood Publishing Group, Inc.
www.lu.com

Printed in the United States of America

The paper used in this book complies with the
Permanent Paper Standard issued by the National
Information Standards Organization (Z39.48–1984).

10 9 8 7 6 5 4 3 2 1

Contents

Acknowledgments

The authors would like to express their appreciation to the Richmond, Virginia, Public Schools, and its superintendent, Dr. Deborah Jewell-Sherman, for their long-standing support of the Mind Games interscholastic competition, from which the ideas in this book grew.

We'd also like to thank our fellow teachers in the RPS Programs for the Gifted, who worked with us through many years of cooperative planning, collegial problem solving, and educational fun. Our supervisors, Anna Lou Schaberg and Rodney Fout, each deserve special, heartfelt thanks for their unflagging support over the years. We couldn't have asked for a stronger pair of advocates for gifted students and for the teachers who serve them.

Thanks to David Odehnal, Mary Ann Ready, and John Hunter for their assistance with the problems in the book and to Elontae Terry who posed for photographs. And thanks to the many educators we've met over the years who have generously shared their ideas with colleagues in classrooms, faculty lounges and workshops. Some of those ideas have undoubtedly found their way into this book, although our faulty memories make it impossible to give proper credit to the people from whom we garnered them.

Most of all, our undying gratitude to Debra Fleisher and Beverly Ziegler, to whom this book is dedicated. They have given us daily support and love, as well as a number of helpful suggestions for this book, taught us virtually everything we know about education, and enriched our lives beyond measure.

Introduction

Every educator wants his or her students to develop skills that allow them to work together cooperatively. We want young people to apply what they've learned as they solve new problems. We want them to be flexible enough to consider a variety of possible answers to open-ended questions. We want them to test and evaluate solutions to a problem rather than jumping on the first "right" answer they come up with. We want students to be willing to tackle difficult problems and to be persistent in their quest to solve them. Most of all, we want them to be excited and enthusiastic about learning.

Skills like these enable students to succeed in real-world situations. But teamwork or enthusiasm can't be taught with drill and practice. You can't promote flexibility by training students to give the "right" answers to standardized multiple-choice tests.

Fortunately, there are other ways to help students develop these skills and attitudes. For more than twenty years, Richmond, Virginia, Public Schools has conducted an annual interscholastic, intellectual competition called Mind Games. This program was instituted by educators in the school system's program for gifted education. On the day of the competition, teams of five students measure themselves against a variety of problem-solving challenges.

We try to involve as many students as possible in the competition. Buses bring students from schools across the city to a central athletic facility. The teams—along with parents, teachers and student cheering sections—dress in their school colors. Each school fields two teams of seven members, five of whom may compete in any one event. Each team is also allowed two additional student "coaches," who help the competitors prepare for the events but will not compete. Some schools even hold intramural competitions several months in advance to determine who will represent their school in the citywide competition.

Teams gather on the bleachers, eager to begin the first of four events. As a team, they answer questions about math, science, language, social studies and current events. They brainstorm multiple answers to open-ended questions. They solve logic puzzles. And in the featured contest of this event, teams present solutions to engineering problems they have worked on for several weeks or more. Finally, as the competition's administrators tally the scores, students lunch on pizza and wait eagerly for the final results. Because we award first through fifth place in each event as well as in overall score, most teams come away with at least one ribbon. But most of all, students all have a huge amount of fun putting their intelligence and creativity to the test.

The problems in this book are based on engineering challenges our students have tackled over the years. The problems are multidisciplinary and open to many possible solutions. They are written to include basic skills from the core curriculum. With the exception of the simplified first challenge, Estimeasurement, they include elements of research and writing, mathematics and science, as well as some sort of artistic presentation such as a skit, a song, or a poem. Each problem requires just a few inexpensive materials and a minimum of equipment.

Although these problems were originally designed for a gifted program, the competition itself should not be limited to students identified as gifted. In fact, the problems give all students the opportunity to display their unique skills and talents. A number of students who later achieved success in the Richmond program for the gifted first "identified themselves" through participation in these competitions. These problems make excellent challenges for intramural as well as interscholastic competitions or for organized gatherings of home-schoolers. They are just as suitable for after-school programs or recreational organizations such as scouts or Boys and Girls Clubs.

Students are often motivated by competition. Nevertheless, we believe cooperation is an equally important human process. It is an essential skill for the modern workplace, where virtually no one tackles a problem individually. Beyond that, if human beings are to continue living together on our little planet, cooperation is a skill we all must learn. We have designed each problem to require cooperative problem solving. To succeed, teams must collaborate, dividing and sharing tasks to work as efficiently as possible. The teams that achieve the greatest success in these problems will be those who learn to work together most effectively.

Mind Builders begins with a few simple exercises that will help students learn to work more effectively in teams. Following that is a selection of ten warm-up problems —short engineering challenges that can be completed within an hour or less, with little advanced preparation. These activities will allow students to practice working together in teams while they solve relatively simple engineering problems.

Finally, the book contains a dozen complete Mind Builders, long-term challenges. These are designed for teams of students to work on for an extended period—as much as a month or two. Much of this work can be done either during after-school activity time, or even during class if the curriculum permits. Individual team members can do some parts of the preparatory work for these challenges at home. The final practices will have to be done as a team. And of course, the competition itself is best conducted in a festive, large-group setting in which each team gets to see the efforts of the others and learn from them.

Each Mind Builder problem includes detailed specifications of the problem's requirements and a scoring rubric. Each team should receive a copy of the rubric when they start work on the challenge. This is very important! Teams should know exactly how they will be scored *before* they begin generating solutions to a problem. Each challenge is also accompanied by suggestions for teachers and coaches and a checklist for administering each competition.

Teams have a spending limit for each problem. This is intended to encourage students to work creatively with simple materials rather than finding a quick solution purchased at an electronics or hardware store. If you find that the $25 limit for these problems is either too limiting or too extravagant, we again encourage you to make appropriate adjustments.

You should expect queries about whether certain techniques are acceptable in solving these problems. Use your best judgment as you consider whether each question meets the spirit as well as the letter of the problem as stated. It is probably wise to keep a written record of these queries and your responses in case other students or coaches have similar inquiries or question your decisions later.

A word about the role of the coach. Coaches and teachers should work as facilitators. Their job is to help students obtain materials, steer them toward the information they need, and supervise teams as they solve the Mind Builders problem. They should make sure the students work safely. Coaches should encourage teams to test their solutions and practice presentations thoroughly before the day of the competition.

It's very important, however, that the solutions belong to the students themselves. Coaches should not solve the problems for the students nor build any devices they might need. That defeats the purpose of these challenges. Good coaching calls for the patience to allow students to learn through their errors, false starts, and interpersonal disputes.

Finally, we encourage anyone using this manual to use it creatively. If you see ways to improve a problem or change it to better fit your needs, please do.

Mind Builders Teamwork

Success with Mind Builders problems requires teamwork. You and your teammates will have to work together effectively to come up with the best possible solution to a problem. But working together isn't always easy. People work at different speeds. They have different ideas—ideas that may conflict with one another.

People also have different styles of attacking a problem. For example, you might like to start by trying out different solutions until you find one that works. One of your teammates may prefer thinking through a variety of possible solutions before actually trying any of them. Someone else might want to start by researching similar problems and the way others have solved them. None of these approaches is "right" or "wrong." They are simply different.

Each Mind Builders problem can be solved in many ways. There is no single "correct" solution, and no one team member has all the answers. It's important to listen to everyone. Your team will be most successful if everyone has a chance to contribute. You have to work as a team.

Teamwork is a skill that can be learned. Knowing how to brainstorm and knowing how to recognize the roles people play as they work in groups will help your team function much more effectively.

Group Roles

When people work together in groups, they play different roles. Learn to observe your group and recognize the various roles people take. This will let you analyze what's missing when the team is not working well and fill missing roles as they are needed. Here are the basic roles every group needs:

Facilitator: Keeps the group running smoothly. Keeps others focused on the group's tasks. Sees that everyone has a chance to contribute and that no one monopolizes the discussion. The facilitator may be elected, but in a small group, the job of facilitator can pass from person to person, informally.

Contributor: Gives ideas, information, or opinions to the group.

Questioner: Asks other members for information or opinions.

Disagreer: Provides a different viewpoint. Disagrees with the opinions of another team member. (Unless a person stands in the way of progress with constant disagreement, this is an important, useful contribution to a group.)

Encourager: Makes other members feel good about their contributions, using words or gestures.

Recorder: Keeps a written record of the group's actions.

Compromiser: Helps disagreeing members come to an agreement.

Clarifier: Summarizes or reviews the important points of a discussion. Helps explain things that others have trouble understanding.

Follower: Goes along with the decisions and actions of the group and helps carry out its tasks.

If you notice your team is missing one of these roles, point it out to the group. Or do the job yourself! Remember, you won't choose just one of these roles to play all the time. You'll play all of them at one time or another. You may be a contributor one minute, a questioner the next, and an encourager the next.

From *Mind Builders: Multidisciplinary Challenges for Cooperative Team-building and Competition* by Paul Fleisher and Donald M. Ziegler. Westport, CT: Libraries Unlimited/Teacher Ideas Press. Copyright © 2006.

Here are a few more roles you should know about—blocking roles. Team members who play these roles sabotage the work of your group.

Blocking Roles

Competitor: Believes he or she always has to be "right" or have the "best" idea. May put other people down.

Monopolizer: Takes more than his or her fair share of the discussion. Often listens poorly to others.

Withdrawer: Allows attention to wander. Does not contribute or participate.

Clown: Uses distracting behaviors to draw attention to himself or herself and away from the team's work.

Learn to recognize blocking roles, and when someone starts to play one of them, ask that person to stop.

When the people on your team have trouble working together, remind yourselves of these group roles. Take some time to practice using them. You *can* learn to work together more effectively. Learning to work as a team can save you many hours of frustration later.

From *Mind Builders: Multidisciplinary Challenges for Cooperative Team-building and Competition* by Paul Fleisher and Donald M. Ziegler. Westport, CT: Libraries Unlimited/Teacher Ideas Press. Copyright © 2006.

Group Roles Practice A

Imagine your class is planning a picnic. Here are some things students might say during the discussion. Identify which role each speaker is playing. (Some roles may appear more than once.)

_____ 1. "First we should set a date and place for the picnic. Then we have to decide on a menu. After that, let's choose some activities for after we eat."

_____ 2. "I think we should go to City Park."

_____ 3. "I don't. Riverside Park has more room and nicer shelters."

_____ 4. "Let's charter a jet plane and fly to Paris!"

_____ 5. "Does anyone know how much it costs to rent a shelter at the park?"

_____ 6. "Okay, we've decided on Riverside Park. Now we should make a menu."

_____ 7. "I think we should have hotdogs. They're easy to cook."

_____ 8. "Not everyone likes hot dogs. I think we should have hamburgers instead."

_____ 9. "How about if we have some of both—hotdogs for the people who like hot dogs, and hamburgers for the kids who like hamburgers."

_____ 10. "That's a great idea!"

_____ 11. "Hotdogs and hamburgers are fine with me."

_____ 12. "I'll write down a list of all the food we'll need for the picnic."

Answer Key: 1. Facilitator; 2. Contributor; 3. Disagreer; 4. Clown; 5. Questioner; 6. Clarifier (or facilitator); 7. Contributor; 8. Disagreer; 9. Compromiser; 10. Encourager; 11. Follower; 12. Recorder

Group Roles Practice B

Imagine your class is planning a field day. Write something each person might say as he or she plays each of the following roles listed:

Facilitator:

_____

Contributor:

_____

Questioner:

_____

Disagreer:

_____

Encourager:

_____

Recorder:

_____

Compromiser:

_____

Clarifier:

_____

Follower:

_____

Competitor:

_____

Monopolizer:

_____

Withdrawer:

_____

Clown:

_____

From _Mind Builders: Multidisciplinary Challenges for Cooperative Team-building and Competition_ by Paul Fleisher and Donald M. Ziegler. Westport, CT: Libraries Unlimited/Teacher Ideas Press. Copyright © 2006.

Group Roles Practice C: The Fishbowl

Pair up with another team. Seat yourselves so one team is sitting in a small circle (in the "fishbowl"). The other team sits in a larger circle surrounding the smaller circle (outside the "fishbowl").

The team in the fishbowl then conducts a 3- to 5-minute discussion. Meanwhile, the outer group observes the discussion. They pay attention to the different roles that the speakers are playing. The outer group can take notes, but they may not speak.

After time is up, the outer group shares its observations and discusses which roles were used and which speakers used them.

Then, the two teams switch positions and repeat the exercise.

Possible topics for discussion could include:

- How to improve the school cafeteria

- How to encourage students to become more physically fit

- How to raise money for (an important charity or school function)

- How to improve life for young people in your community

- How to prepare for a successful future

From *Mind Builders: Multidisciplinary Challenges for Cooperative Team-building and Competition* by Paul Fleisher and Donald M. Ziegler. Westport, CT: Libraries Unlimited/Teacher Ideas Press. Copyright © 2006.

Brainstorming

Brainstorming is a way to gather lots of good ideas quickly. When you brainstorm, follow these few simple rules:

1. **Don't judge!** Your goal is to collect as many ideas as possible. You'll have time to decide which ideas are best later. If someone in the group is judging ideas, remind them that you will evaluate the ideas *after* you finish brainstorming.

2. **Work quickly.** As soon as you collect one idea, move on to the next. You'll have time to elaborate on the best ideas later.

3. **Work out loud.** When you have an idea, say it. Brainstorming works best when people build on each other's ideas. This is called piggybacking. Hearing one idea often triggers new and different ideas from other team members.

4. **Speak up.** You can't piggyback on an idea you haven't heard. If you miss something a teammate has said, ask them to repeat it.

5. **Write down every idea.** One of your team members should serve as a recorder. Even if an idea sounds silly, write it down. Remember, you'll select the best ideas later.

6. **Keep going.** When you think you've run out of ideas, think a little longer. Some of your best ideas may come at the end, after you think you're finished.

When the team has finished brainstorming, your next task is to evaluate. Go through the ideas you've generated. Throw out the ones that won't work, or are impractical or silly.

Talk about the ones you think might be best. Think about them some more. Elaborate on them—add details. Consider possible problems or difficulties each good idea might bring. Combine ideas. Maybe two or three of your brainstorms can work together.

Then, make your decision. Choose the idea you think is the very best. But don't throw the list of other ideas away. You may want to use them later.

From *Mind Builders: Multidisciplinary Challenges for Cooperative Team-building and Competition* by Paul Fleisher and Donald M. Ziegler. Westport, CT: Libraries Unlimited/Teacher Ideas Press. Copyright © 2006.

Brainstorming Practice

Review the brainstorming process. Then give teams one of the objects listed below. Having the actual object in front of them as they do their brainstorming will help teams generate ideas more effectively.

Their instructions are to think of as many different and creative uses for the object as they can in 10 minutes. Teams should generate a large list of possibilities, other than the use for which the object was originally intended. Remind students to avoid making judgments on the ideas during the 10-minute period.

After 10 minutes, give teams an additional 5 minutes to select their 10 best ideas. Teams should select for variety as well as originality. For example, suppose the object they are working with is a paper clip. If the team selects hanging a plant, hanging up a calendar, and hanging a picture, those are really only a single idea.

Objects for Brainstorming Practice

paper clip	dryer vent hose
toothpick	wooden barbeque skewer
o ring	comb
hose washer	sunglasses
plastic tubing	claw staple remover
plastic garbage bag	c-clamp
used CD	folding carpenter's rule
washer	bungee cord
plastic cup	cassette tape case
bicycle inner tube	hose clamp
twist tie	snail shell
gum eraser	pinecone
pencil	carabiner
colander	film canister
3 x 5 card	pipe cleaner
length of string	large Q-tip
length of wire	tongue depressor

From *Mind Builders: Multidisciplinary Challenges for Cooperative Team-building and Competition* by Paul Fleisher and Donald M. Ziegler. Westport, CT: Libraries Unlimited/Teacher Ideas Press. Copyright © 2006.

Warm-up Problems

Teachers' Guidelines

Teamwork: The following warm-ups are intended to give students practice in both problem solving and teamwork. They are written for five-person teams. However, if students are having difficulty working cooperatively, the problems can be used with smaller teams of two to three individuals at first. Encourage students to work with a variety of partners. One of the goals of these activities is for students to discover which partners they work with effectively and which partnerships create distractions or result in conflicts. You may decide to assign teams if students have difficulty switching partners.

Materials: The everyday materials required for these challenges should be easy to obtain. Make sure you have them assembled and separated by team on the day of the activity. Encourage kids to use their materials creatively. We once gave students a construction problem, along with a bag full of materials. One team asked the question, "Can we use the bag?" We hadn't considered the bag itself one of the materials on our list. Our answer: "Of course you can." To reward that team's creative thinking, we did not announce their idea to the other teams in the competition.

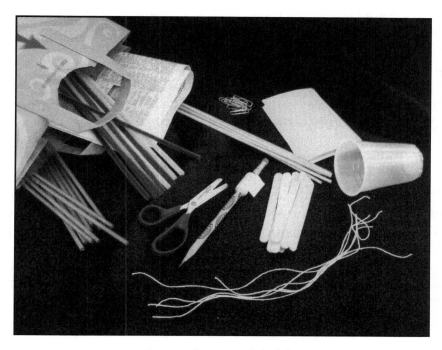

A sample materials kit.

Planning: Have students spend several minutes brainstorming possible solutions and planning how they will attack the problem *before* they begin any work on the problem itself. Otherwise, they are likely to make false starts and misuse their limited supply of materials.

Level of Difficulty: We've attempted to present the warm-up problems in order of their level of difficulty, from easiest to most difficult. We recommend starting students with easier problems and working up to the harder ones. However, you are the best judge of your students' abilities. Present these problems to your students in the order that seems most appropriate.

Time Limits: Rather than specify time limits for each problem, we've left a blank for you to set a time that suits your own schedule. However, construction problems require a minimum of 30 minutes to complete; 45 minutes to an hour would probably be preferable. Other problems, such as the prime number or cube folding problem, can be completed in a shorter time.

Balanced Decision Making in Solving Engineering Challenges

Decision making sometimes requires a trade-off. One desired outcome may have to be reduced so that another aspect is maximized. For example, a young couple might plan a long trip on which they eat cheaply and stay in inexpensive lodgings or camp, or they might prefer taking a shorter vacation in luxurious and expensive accommodations.

In many of the challenges that follow, students will have to choose which of two contradictory outcomes they wish to emphasize. A bridge might be constructed to be very long but not so sturdy or very strong but much shorter, for example. Balancing one outcome against another provokes interesting discussion and decision making as teams plan solutions to their engineering challenges.

In many of the following problems, there will be more than one criterion for judging the completed project. The problem may call for a structure that will be measured for both size and the ability to bear weight. In our experience, most teams will try to make their structure as tall or as long as possible. Teams rarely take advantage of the opportunity to sacrifice a strong measurement in one dimension to achieve a higher score in another.

For instance a team might decide to build a very short yet very strong and stable tower capable of holding the maximum amount of weight. Or they might decide to build a very tall tower that would earn many points for height, yet earn none for load bearing. However, creating a solution that puts some emphasis on each of those criteria, rather than placing all the emphasis on one or the other, might result in a better overall score.

Encourage your teams to study the scoring procedure carefully. They should note whether their solution might earn a higher score if they balance both criteria differently.

Building for Strength and Stability

Students may need some guidance as they attempt to discover how to make their structures sturdy and strong. One of the essential principles of structural design is the use of trusses—triangular bracing.

It's easy to demonstrate the relative strength and stability of square and triangular building elements. String a thread through four straws and tie it tight, so you have made a square frame. Make a similar frame with three straws. Let students compare the stability and strength of the two structures. As they manipulate them, they'll see that the triangular frame maintains its shape, while the square is easily deformed.

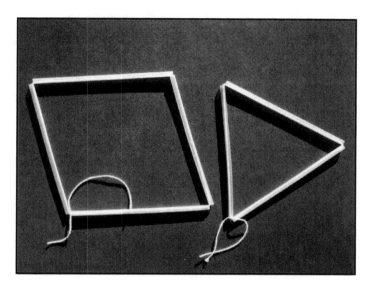

Square and triangular building elements.

You may also make test frames using toothpicks and balls of modeling clay, gum-drops, or mini-marshmallows.

Students may experiment with the straw structures by adding diagonal bracing or by adding a tight skin of glued tissue paper.

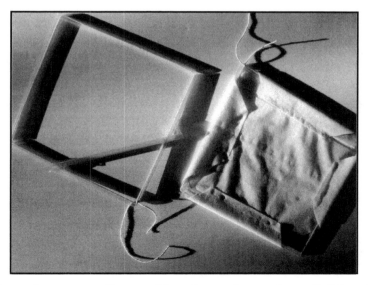

Braced squares: diagonal bracing using a straw (left) and bracing using a skin of tissue paper glued to the square.

These principles extend into three dimensions as well. Add a straw to your triangle at each of the three vertices. Join their opposite ends to form a four-sided triangular solid—a tetrahedron.

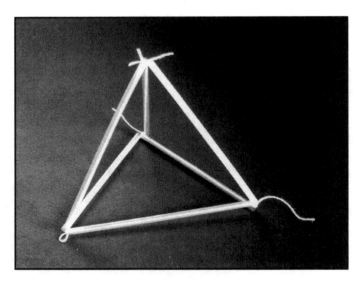

A tetrahedron.

For comparison, make a cube by extending your square into 3 dimensions. Students will find that the cube deforms easily, while the tetrahedron maintains a rigid shape. Ask what they could add to the cube to make it rigid.

Alexander Graham Bell, inventor of the telephone, was also known for his experiments with the tetrahedron. Bell was impressed with its strength and rigidity. He joined many tetrahedra together to build kites that could lift a person. (You, too, can make excellent kites by covering two sides of your structure with a tight paper skin.)

Inherent Limitations

As students build towers, bridges, and other structures, they will discover there is a limit imposed by the materials themselves. When the weight of the structure itself reaches a certain point, it will collapse as materials or joints begin to fail. A structure always fails at its weakest point. As students test their structures, they should note *where* they fail. This may help them strengthen weak points and improve the structure's performance in future trials.

Prime Time

The Challenge: Make a list of as many prime numbers as you can identify, in order, within the given time limit.

Directions: A prime number is any number greater than 1 that is only divisible by itself and by 1. The first four prime numbers are 2, 3, 5, and 7.

Your task is to list all the prime numbers, as high as you can go. You will receive **one point** for each prime number you list correctly. However, you will lose **two points** for

- each number on your list that is not a prime number.

- each prime number below your highest number that you omit from in the list.

Each team may use no more than two electronic calculators as you work on the problems. Other team members may calculate using paper and pencil as needed.

Before you begin your list, plan a strategy for your team to use as you attack the problem.

When time is called, your team must present a single list of prime numbers to be judged.

Materials: paper, pencils, two calculators per team

Judge's equipment: Stopwatch or clock, answer key (list of prime numbers)

From *Mind Builders: Multidisciplinary Challenges for Cooperative Team-building and Competition* by Paul Fleisher and Donald M. Ziegler. Westport, CT: Libraries Unlimited/Teacher Ideas Press. Copyright © 2006.

Answer Key: Prime numbers below 3,000

2 3 5 7 11 13 17 19 23 29 31 37 41 43 47 53 59 61 67 71 73 79 83 89 97 101 103 107 109 113 127 131 137 139 149 151 157 163 167 173 179 181 191 193 197 199 211 223 227 229 233 239 241 251 257 263 269 271 277 281 283 293 307 311 313 317 331 337 347 349 353 359 367 373 379 383 389 397 401 409 419 421 431 433 439 443 449 457 461 463 467 479 487 491 499 503 509 521 523 541 547 557 563 569 571 577 587 593 599 601 607 613 617 619 631 641 643 647 653 659 661 673 677 683 691 701 709 719 727 733 739 743 751 757 761 769 773 787 797 809 811 821 823 827 829 839 853 857 859 863 877 881 883 887 907 911 919 929 937 941 947 953 967 971 977 983 991 997 1009 1013 1019 1021 1031 1033 1039 1049 1051 1061 1063 1069 1087 1091 1093 1097 1103 1109 1117 1123 1129 1151 1153 1163 1171 1181 1187 1193 1201 1213 1217 1223 1229 1231 1237 1249 1259 1277 1279 1283 1289 1291 1297 1301 1303 1307 1319 1321 1327 1361 1367 1373 1381 1399 1409 1423 1427 1429 1433 1439 1447 1451 1453 1459 1471 1481 1483 1487 1489 1493 1499 1511 1523 1531 1543 1549 1553 1559 1567 1571 1579 1583 1597 1601 1607 1609 1613 1619 1621 1627 1637 1657 1663 1667 1669 1693 1697 1699 1709 1721 1723 1733 1741 1747 1753 1759 1777 1783 1787 1789 1801 1811 1823 1831 1847 1861 1867 1871 1873 1877 1879 1889 1901 1907 1913 1931 1933 1949 1951 1973 1979 1987 1993 1997 1999 2003 2011 2017 2027 2029 2039 2053 2063 2069 2081 2083 2087 2089 2099 2111 2113 2129 2131 2137 2141 2143 2153 2161 2179 2203 2207 2213 2221 2237 2239 2243 2251 2267 2269 2273 2281 2287 2293 2297 2309 2311 2333 2339 2341 2347 2351 2357 2371 2377 2381 2383 2389 2393 2399 2411 2417 2423 2437 2441 2447 2459 2467 2473 2477 2503 2521 2531 2539 2543 2549 2551 2557 2579 2591 2593 2609 2617 2621 2633 2647 2657 2659 2663 2671 2677 2683 2687 2689 2693 2699 2707 2711 2713 2719 2729 2731 2741 2749 2753 2767 2777 2789 2791 2797 2801 2803 2819 2833 2837 2843 2851 2857 2861 2879 2887 2897 2903 2909 2917 2927 2939 2953 2957 2963 2969 2971 2999

Longer lists of prime numbers are readily available on the Internet.

From *Mind Builders: Multidisciplinary Challenges for Cooperative Team-building and Competition* by Paul Fleisher and Donald M. Ziegler. Westport, CT: Libraries Unlimited/Teacher Ideas Press. Copyright © 2006.

Newspaper Skyscraper

The Challenge: Using only 12 full sheets of newspaper and 1 meter of masking tape, create the tallest possible self-supporting structure.

Directions: Collect your materials. Set them aside while you plan how to solve the problem. You may use pencils and notebook paper to plan your design. You *will not* be issued replacement materials if you damage what you have been given or change plans after you've start work on the problem.

Team members may stand on a chair as they construct the tower. They may *not* stand on any other objects.

When construction is completed, the tower must be self-supporting. That is, it must stand up by itself, without any assistance from either people or other objects. It must remain standing for at least 30 seconds without any support.

The tower will be judged on its vertical height only, as measured from the highest point above the floor. Each team will have its tower measured only once. You may ask to have your tower judged at any point before time has expired. When time expires, all remaining towers will be measured as they stand at that moment.

Masking tape may be used only on the newspaper itself, or to attach newspaper to the floor. You may not use tape to attach the tower to walls or furniture.

Materials: 12 full sheets of newspaper, 1 meter of masking tape, scissors, notebook paper, and pencil (for planning purposes only)

Judge's equipment: tape measure, stepladder, clock or stopwatch

From *Mind Builders: Multidisciplinary Challenges for Cooperative Team-building and Competition* by Paul Fleisher and Donald M. Ziegler. Westport, CT: Libraries Unlimited/Teacher Ideas Press. Copyright © 2006.

Paper Bridges

The Challenge: Create a bridge out of a single 8.5 x 11 inch sheet of plain paper that will support the greatest load.

Directions: Place two bricks exactly 6 inches apart. The bricks will serve as the piers (supports) for your bridge.

Using a single sheet of plain paper, design a bridge that will rest across the two piers. You may bend, cut, fold or otherwise modify the paper. You may not use any other materials for the bridge span, however.

Pennies will serve as the standard load for your bridge. Test the bridge by placing pennies on the span between the two piers. All pennies must be placed between the two piers. No pennies may be placed so that they are supported by the brick beneath the paper.

Bridge failure occurs when the bridge collapses. When the bridge fails, carefully count the number of pennies the bridge was able to support. Do *not* count the last penny or pennies added—the ones that caused the bridge to collapse.

You may try as many bridge designs as you like during the allotted time, using a fresh sheet of paper each time. Your final score will be the number of pennies supported by your best bridge design.

Materials: 8.5 x 11 inch copier paper, scissors, two bricks per team, ruler or ruled grid paper (for placement of bricks), pennies

Judge's equipment: timer, large supply of pennies

Time Limit: _____

Paper Bridges 2

The Challenge: Create the longest possible self-supporting bridge stretching between two desks, using only 12 sheets of newspaper.

Directions: Collect your materials. Set them aside while you plan how to solve the problem. Plan the design for your bridge *before* you begin building. You may use pencils and notebook paper to draw your design. You may also experiment with different ways to join sheets of paper together using the notebook paper.

You *will not* be issued replacement materials if you damage what you have been given or change plans after you start work on the problem.

When construction is completed, the bridge must be self-supporting. That is, it must not touch or be held up by any other object or person. It must remain intact and above the floor for at least 30 seconds without any support.

The bridge will be judged only by its length, as measured between the two closest points on the desks that serve as its piers. Each team will have its bridge measured only once. You may ask to have the bridge judged before time expires. When time expires, all remaining bridges will be measured as they stand at that moment. Bridges that do not successfully span a gap between two desks will receive 0 points.

Materials: 12 full sheets of newspaper, two textbooks, notebook paper and pencils

Judge's equipment: Measuring tape, stopwatch or clock

Time Limit: _____

Clay Boat

Your task is to use a 4-ounce stick of modeling clay to make a boat. The boat must float in water and be able to carry as much weight as possible before sinking or tipping over.

There will be a 5-minute period for you to examine the materials and to plan. At the end of 5 minutes, the construction period will begin. You may test your boat in a water-filled pan. Please use a paper towel to carry it back to your table.

Select one person from your team to serve as the Loader. That person will carefully place weights into the boat one at a time when it is judged.

Scoring:

- Points will be given for completion of a floating clay boat.

- Points will be given for the number of weights the boat can hold before it sinks or tips over.

You may place a maximum of 20 weights in your boat.
Cooperate, plan carefully, build well, and may your load stay dry.

Clay Boat Judging Form

1. **Presentation** of boat that floats (10 points)   _____

2. **Load Bearing**

Number of weights held at sinking or tipping of boat _____ x 5 = _____

(If the seventh weight tips or sinks the boat, multiply **6** by 5, and enter 30 in the tally column.)

(Maximum number of weights = 20)

Total Score [   ]

From *Mind Builders: Multidisciplinary Challenges for Cooperative Team-building and Competition* by Paul Fleisher and Donald M. Ziegler. Westport, CT: Libraries Unlimited/Teacher Ideas Press. Copyright © 2006.

Clay Boat Coaches Hints

You may encourage students to study various boat shapes before the competition.

Test the clay material before the competition. Buy non-hardening, oil-based modeling clay. In the interest of saving money, we once bought the least expensive clay available. It turned out to be water soluble. Student vessels turned into a muddy mess, which was hilarious only in retrospect.

Have several water-filled pans available for students to test their boat designs before they present them for judging.

Set up a judging pond. Use a basin or other water container large enough and deep enough to float all possible shapes of boats. Place the container on floor level. Cover the area with a waterproof tarp.

Students should place the weights on the boat themselves. Heavy washers, hex nuts, or 1-inch carriage bolts (all available at any hardware store) make good weights. We recommend against using fishing weights because they are made of lead.

Instruct the students to place the weights carefully in the boat, one at a time. After judging, teams should take their boats away with a paper towel to prevent dripping.

Judges may begin judging before the half-hour construction period is finished, as soon as a team brings its completed boat to the judging pond.

Materials: Modeling clay, large basin, water, standard weights, paper towels, plastic tarp

From *Mind Builders: Multidisciplinary Challenges for Cooperative Team-building and Competition* by Paul Fleisher and Donald M. Ziegler. Westport, CT: Libraries Unlimited/Teacher Ideas Press. Copyright © 2006.

Folding a Cube

The Challenge: A cube has six sides. Each side is a square. Some arrangements of six connected squares can be folded to form a cube. Others cannot. For example:

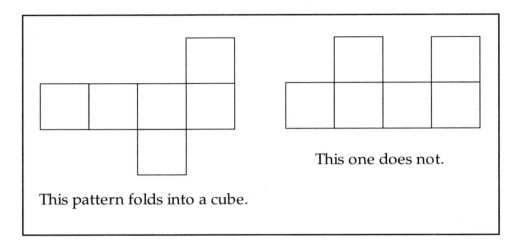

This pattern folds into a cube.

This one does not.

Using grid paper, produce as many *different* arrangements of six squares that can be folded into a square. Once that has been completed, find and produce as many *different* arrangements of squares that can be folded into a rectangular solid.

Directions:

1. On grid paper, outline as many different arrangements of six squares that can be folded into a cube as you can think of, using pencil and ruler. (There are a limited number of correct answers.) Cut out each arrangement and fold to check. Put each arrangement aside for judging. Your team will earn 1 point for each arrangement that can be folded into a cube. You will lose 2 points for each arrangement that cannot be folded into a cube.

2. Next, outline as many arrangements of 10 squares as you can think of that can be folded into a rectangular solid that is two squares long and one square wide. (This problem has more possible solutions.) Cut out each arrangement and fold to check. Put each arrangement aside for judging as it is completed. You will earn 2 points for each different arrangement that can be folded into a rectangular solid. You will lose 3 points for each arrangement you present that cannot.

Materials: Grid paper, ruler, pencil, scissors

Judge's equipment: Answer key, stopwatch or clock

From *Mind Builders: Multidisciplinary Challenges for Cooperative Team-building and Competition* by Paul Fleisher and Donald M. Ziegler. Westport, CT: Libraries Unlimited/Teacher Ideas Press. Copyright © 2006.

Answer key for cube patterns

A few patterns that will make a double cube. There are more.

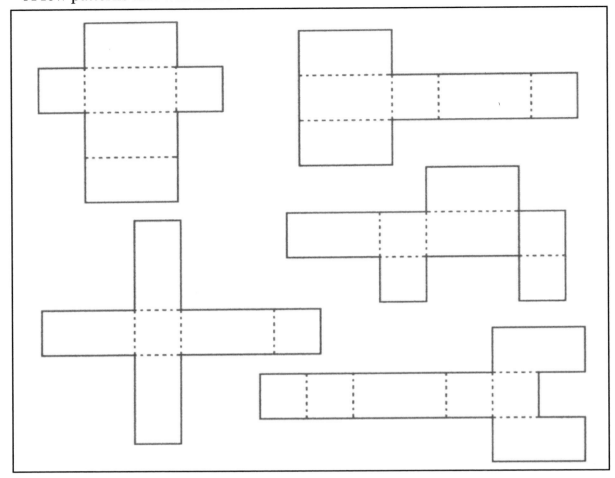

Bottle Emptying

You will be given two capped 1-liter plastic soda bottles full of water. You will also have four straws, a pair of scissors, a length of plastic tubing, 1 meter of duct tape rolled on a pencil, a plastic dishpan, and a funnel.

The purpose of the contest is to see who can empty their bottle the fastest. You may alter or hold the bottle any way you like. **There will be no access to more water during the practice or the judging period.**

At the end of the practice period, you will bring one bottle filled with water to the judging area. There will be a penalty if the bottle is not completely full. At a signal, empty the bottle as quickly as you can. The time for complete emptying will be recorded, and you will be given points accordingly.

Scoring

- The time it takes to empty the bottle will be measured in seconds. Your score will be 100 minus the number of seconds it takes to empty the bottle.

- At the time of judging, the bottle filled with water will be weighed. For each ounce less than the original full bottle measurement, 1 point will be deducted.

Cooperate, plan carefully, and test various techniques. Try to stay as dry as possible.

Score: 100 – _____	– _____	= _____
seconds to empty bottle	missing oz. of water	

Non-Leaning Tower of Peanut Butter

Construct a tall, strong tower using the materials in your construction kit. You must build a cup onto the top of the tower to hold weights that will test the tower's strength.

The judge will measure the height of the tower. To test your tower's strength, you will then place weights into the cup one at a time until the tower or the cup collapses.

You will earn points for

- **completing a tower with a cup mounted at the top.**

- **making the tower as tall as possible, measured to the top of the cup.**

- **adding weights to the cup until the tower collapses.**

You will have 5 minutes to examine the materials and plan your construction. You may not begin construction until the 5-minute period is over. You may draw diagrams or write the steps for your work if you wish. Plan well, cooperate, and do not eat your building materials.

Each team will have its tower measured only once. You may ask to have the tower judged at any point before time expires. When time expires, all remaining towers will be judged as they stand at that moment.

Materials: one 4-oz. sleeve of saltine crackers, one 6-oz. jar of creamy peanut butter, one small plastic cup, one tongue depressor for each member of the team (not to be used as part of the structure)

Scoring:

1. Completion of tower (10 points) _____

2. Total height of tower (1 point per cm) _____

3. Number of weights held at collapse x 5 = _____

Total ⬛⬛⬛⬛

Coaches Hints for Peanut Butter Tower

Begin judging as soon as a team indicates it has completed its work. The judge will measure the height of the tower from its base to the top of the cup. Enter the number of centimeters on line 2. Then allow a student to place weights into the cup, one by one. When the tower collapses or sags so that the cup falls, enter the number of weights held prior to collapse. Multiply this number by 5 and enter on line 3.

Heavy washers, hex nuts, or 1-inch carriage bolts (all available at a hardware store) make good weights. We recommend against using lead fishing weights.

Several years ago we used this problem in a competition for second and third graders. As the students worked, we were dismayed to see that many teams were discreetly watching how neighboring teams were tackling the problem. Only one or two teams had used the saltines on edge, vertically. Those structures were abandoned as unstable. The solution that quickly spread among the teams was stacking the mortared crackers, sandwich style, in a messy yet stable tower. The result was an assortment of multilayered peanut butter cracker sandwiches, all approximately the same height, depending on the thickness of the peanut butter mortar.

As practice for the peanut butter tower, teams might experiment with making a house of cards. Builders would use a deck of ordinary playing cards to build as tall a tower as possible. Some might discover that cards in groups of three leaning slightly inward in a triangular arrangement present a relatively stable arrangement. With care a couple of cards can be placed on the triangular base to make a flat roof. Another triangular structure can then be built on this foundation. Such a delicate tower can be built as high as students' trembling hands and air currents allow.

A House of Cards.

Tower of Pasta

Construct a tall, strong tower using the materials in your construction kit. You must build a cup into your tower, at least 10 centimeters above the base of the tower. Continue building the tower above and beyond the cup as high as you can. You can make the base of the tower as wide as you want, but no points will be given for width.

You will have 5 minutes to examine the materials and plan your construction. Do not begin to put the materials together until the end of the 5 minutes. You may draw diagrams or write plans if you wish. Plan well, cooperate, build strong, build tall, and have fun!

You may request that your tower be judged as soon as it is completed. At the time of judging, the minimum cup height will be checked. The total height of the tower will be measured. To test your tower's strength, you will place weights into the cup one at a time until the tower or the cup collapses.

Materials:

- one package of dry spaghetti (note: use thick spaghetti, not vermicelli or spaghettini)

- one package of gumdrops or mini-marshmallows

- weights (washers, hex nuts, or carriage bolts)

Tower of Pasta Judging Form

1. Completion of tower (10 points)   _____

2. Cup bottom measures at least 10 cm from base (10 points)   _____

3. Total height of tower (1 point per cm)   _____

4. Number of weights held before collapse x 5 =   _____

Total [   ]

From *Mind Builders: Multidisciplinary Challenges for Cooperative Team-building and Competition* by Paul Fleisher and Donald M. Ziegler. Westport, CT: Libraries Unlimited/Teacher Ideas Press. Copyright © 2006.

Time Limit: _____

Strong Shelf

Use any or all of the materials to build a shelf attached to the wall. You may use only the tape provided to attach your shelf to the wall. No part of the shelf may touch the floor. Somewhere on this shelf you must attach a cup that will be used to hold weights to measure the strength of the shelf.

You *will not* be issued replacement materials if you damage what you have been given or change plans after you start work on the problem.

There will be a 5-minute period for you to examine the materials and plan. You may request that your shelf be judged as soon as it is completed. Cooperate, plan carefully, build well, and may gravity be your friend.

Scoring: You will earn points for

- completion of a shelf attached to the wall, which supports the cup.

- the distance of the cup from the wall.

- the number of weights the cup can hold before shelf collapse.

Strong Shelf Judging Form

Presentation of shelf mounted on wall holding a cup (10 points)   _____

Horizontal distance of cup from wall surface   _____

(10 points for each centimeter, measured to closest edge of cup)

Number of weights held before collapse   _____ x 5 = _____

(If the seventh weight collapses the shelf, multiply **6** by 5, and enter 30 in the tally column.)

(Maximum number of weights = 10)   Total [   ]

From *Mind Builders: Multidisciplinary Challenges for Cooperative Team-building and Competition* by Paul Fleisher and Donald M. Ziegler. Westport, CT: Libraries Unlimited/Teacher Ideas Press. Copyright © 2006.

Materials to include in kit:

　　1 meter length of duct tape wound around a pencil

　　1 scissors (not to be a part of the construction)

　　1 wire coat hanger

　　10 plastic soda straws

　　1 plastic cup, 8-ounce, to hold the weights

　　4 index cards (3 x 5")

　　10 pipe cleaners

　　6 pieces of string, 1 foot long each

　　12 medium-size paper clips

　　8 wooden skewers

　　1 sheet of newspaper

　　12 popsicle sticks

Advice to coaches:

In this problem, each team must decide whether to place the cup a great distance from the wall, which will support fewer weights, or a short distance, supporting more weights.

Make sure that it is OK with building authorities to mount shelves to the wall with duct tape. Some schools do not allow tape on walls. In this case, a smooth vertical surface—such as plywood or foam core board—can be provided. (GOO GONE can remove tape glue remaining on surfaces.)

Heavy washers, hex nuts, or 1-inch carriage bolts (all available at a hardware store) make good weights. We recommend against using lead fishing weights.

Judges may begin judging as soon as a team is ready. Judges should circulate during construction period to remind teams, if necessary, that no part of the shelf can touch the floor.

From *Mind Builders: Multidisciplinary Challenges for Cooperative Team-building and Competition* by Paul Fleisher and Donald M. Ziegler. Westport, CT: Libraries Unlimited/Teacher Ideas Press. Copyright © 2006.

Mind Builders Long-Term Challenges

Administrators' Checklist
(Applicable for all long-term competitions)

Setting up a Mind Builders competition requires organizational work to ensure the event goes smoothly. You'll need to find a time and place for the event, recruit and meet with coaches or teachers, gather materials, find judges, and make any number of other preparations. Of course, like any similar project, the first time is the hardest. After you've done it once, the preparation becomes much easier, even though the actual problem may be different each time.

The following checklist will be helpful for anyone preparing and administering a Mind Builders competition.

Advanced Planning:

_____ Set the location, date, and time for competition.

_____ Arrange for student transportation to and from competition site, if needed.

_____ Determine number of participating teams, team members, and coaches.

_____ Obtain supplies and materials to be provided to students for the competition.

_____ Distribute copies of the problem, scoring rubric, and any standard materials to each coach.

_____ Produce or obtain certificates for all participating students and coaches.

_____ Identify, recruit, and invite volunteers to judge the competition.

_____ Obtain trophies, ribbons, or other awards for winning teams.

_____ Produce and distribute news releases publicizing the competition (optional).

Two Weeks Prior to the Competition:

_____ Confirm competition location.

_____ Confirm volunteer judges. Arrange for them to arrive early enough for training.

From *Mind Builders: Multidisciplinary Challenges for Cooperative Team-building and Competition* by Paul Fleisher and Donald M. Ziegler. Westport, CT: Libraries Unlimited/Teacher Ideas Press. Copyright © 2006.

_____ Assign a cleanup crew to put things back in order after the competition.

_____ Remind local media about the competition (optional).

Arrange for the following equipment/supplies to be available on the day of the competition:

_____ Tables to exhibit students' research displays.

_____ Seating for participants, coaches, and spectators.

_____ Multiple copies of the scoring rubric.

_____ Copies of the problem description for each judge.

_____ Two stopwatches (one for backup).

_____ PA system with one or more microphones for student performances.

_____ Pens, pencils, and masking tape.

_____ Clipboards for judges.

_____ Electronic calculators for computing scores.

_____ A computerized spreadsheet to record and sort scores (optional).

_____ Snacks and drinks (optional).

On the Day of the Competition:

_____ Set up tables and chairs for displays and for spectators.

_____ Reserve chairs for the judges at the front of the audience.

_____ Set up and test PA system.

_____ Put furniture and other materials needed for the competition in place.

_____ Train judges. Explain their tasks, including assessing displays, evaluating performances, and assessing the results of the engineering challenge. Review scoring sheets with them.

_____ Prepare ribbons and trophies for distribution.

_____ Conduct random drawing to establish the order in which teams will compete.

From _Mind Builders: Multidisciplinary Challenges for Cooperative Team-building and Competition_ by Paul Fleisher and Donald M. Ziegler. Westport, CT: Libraries Unlimited/Teacher Ideas Press. Copyright © 2006.

EstiMeasurement

It's often important to know just how warm, how heavy, or how long an object is. But we don't always have a measuring device with us. Even if we do, we have to be able to tell if we are measuring correctly, and if the measuring device itself is accurate. So we need a good understanding of our units of measurement. This challenge will require you to know the size of a variety of standard units of measurement.

The Challenge: Your team will be required to estimate a variety of measurements, using nothing but your own brains and bodies. You will be asked to estimate lengths—in both centimeters and meters; duration—in seconds; volume—in milliliters and liters; mass—in both grams and kilograms; and temperature—in degrees Celsius.

To prepare for this challenge, you team will have to familiarize itself with these various units of measurement and devise strategies to estimate measurements with them. The more accurate your estimates are at the competition, the more points your team will score.

At the competition, you will be given a stick. You must estimate its length in centimeters. You will be shown another length, marked on the floor. You will estimate that length in meters.

You will be given a container of water. You must estimate the volume of the water in milliliters. And you will be given a cardboard box to estimate its volume in liters.

You will be given another container of water, with a temperature somewhere between 0 and 35 degrees Celsius. You will be asked to estimate the temperature.

You will be given a small weight and a large weight. You must estimate the mass of the first in grams and the second in kilograms.

Your team will record each estimate on an answer sheet. **You will have no more than 3 minutes to complete all the estimates listed above.**

Finally, you will be asked to estimate a period of time lasting somewhere between 30 and 90 seconds.

Using parts of your body in the process of estimation is acceptable. However, no other items, including clothing, may be used to assist in your estimates.

Note: If you are not certain whether a particular technique is acceptable, check with an adult sponsor *before* the day of the competition.

From *Mind Builders: Multidisciplinary Challenges for Cooperative Team-building and Competition* by Paul Fleisher and Donald M. Ziegler. Westport, CT: Libraries Unlimited/Teacher Ideas Press. Copyright © 2006.

Like Leonardo da Vinci, students can explore the measurements and proportions of the human figure.

EstiMeasurement

Answer Sheet

Length of stick: _____ cm

Length of floor distance: _____ m

Volume of water: _____ ml

Volume of cardboard box: _____ l

Temperature of water: _____ °C

Mass of small weight: _____ g

Mass of large weight: _____ kg

Time estimate:

Requested length of time: _____ sec

Team's actual estimate: _____ sec

From *Mind Builders: Multidisciplinary Challenges for Cooperative Team-building and Competition* by Paul Fleisher and Donald M. Ziegler. Westport, CT: Libraries Unlimited/Teacher Ideas Press. Copyright © 2006.

EstiMeasurement

Scoring Sheet

Team _____

Length of stick:

Actual: _____ cm   Estimate: _____ cm   Difference: _____   Score: _____

Score = 25 pts. – 1 pt. for each centimeter above or below actual length

Length of floor distance:

Actual: _____ m   Estimate: _____ m   Difference: _____   Score: _____

Score = 25 pts. – 1 pt. for each meter above or below actual length

Volume of water:

Actual: _____ ml   Estimate: _____ ml   Difference: _____   Score: _____

Score = 25 pts. – 1 pt. for each 10 ml (or portion thereof) above or below actual volume

Volume of cardboard box:

Actual: _____ l   Estimate: _____ l   Difference: _____   Score: _____

Score = 25 pts. – 1 pt. for each (or portion thereof) above or below actual volume

Temperature of water:

Actual: _____ C   Estimate: _____ C   Difference: _____   Score: _____

Score = 25 pts. – 1 pt. for each °C above or below actual temperature

Mass of small weight:

Actual: _____ g   Estimate: _____ g   Difference: _____   Score: _____

Score = 25 pts. – 1 pt. for each 5 g (or portion thereof) above or below actual mass

Mass of large weight:

Actual: _____ kg   Estimate: _____ kg   Difference: _____   Score: _____

Score = 25 pts. – 1 pt. for each kg (or portion thereof) above or below actual mass

Time estimate:

Actual: _____ sec   Estimate: _____ sec   Difference: _____   Score: _____

Score = 25 pts. – 1 pt. for each second above or below requested time.

Total [_____]

EstiMeasurement

Hints for Coaches

Success for students in this challenge is most of all a matter of practice. Team members should practice estimating the various measurements repeatedly and then check those estimates with the appropriate measuring devices.

Teams will probably discover that some members are better at estimating certain measurements than others. For example, one team member may excel at estimating length, while another is better at estimating mass. At that point, individual team members may decide to "specialize" in particular estimates.

Using body parts to aid in estimating *is* acceptable. For example, a student may discover that his finger is approximately one centimeter wide, or that his arm span is about two meters in length. Using any other object, including clothing, as an aid to making the estimates is *not* allowed.

The team will also have to plan a strategy for completing all estimates (except time) within the 3-minute time limit. This may call for dividing up the estimates among team members. There is no requirement that all estimates be done by all team members.

Teams may find it valuable to "check" one another's estimates. For example, two members may be assigned to estimate volume. They may choose to make independent estimates, then compare results and agree on a final answer. Or they may decide to agree on a single answer cooperatively, through discussion.

From *Mind Builders: Multidisciplinary Challenges for Cooperative Team-building and Competition* by Paul Fleisher and Donald M. Ziegler. Westport, CT: Libraries Unlimited/Teacher Ideas Press. Copyright © 2006.

EstiMeasurement

Administrators' Checklist

In addition to the standard Administrators' Checklist, this problem requires the following preparations:

Advanced Planning:

Assemble the following materials:

_____ Meter stick or metric tape measure

_____ Several dowels of different lengths, ranging from 35 to 75 cm: Mark each with a different letter (A, B, C, etc.) Measure each dowel and record lengths on an "answer key."

_____ Several large cardboard boxes: Seal with tape. Label with letters, measure, and calculate volume in liters. Record. (1 liter = 1000 cubic centimeters)

_____ Several small items ranging in mass from 100 to 250 g: Label, measure on a balance or scale, and record.

_____ Several heavier items ranging in mass from 5 to 15 kg: Label, measure on a balance or scale, and record.

_____ A large plastic bowl or other container that can hold water

_____ A graduated measuring cup that can measure amounts between 250 and 750 ml

_____ A clean 5-gallon plastic bucket to serve as a water reservoir

_____ Two large insulated thermos jugs to hold hot and cold water

_____ Large Styrofoam cups for testing water temperature (Double the cups for extra insulation.)

_____ A Celsius thermometer

_____ Copies of answer sheets and scoring sheets

On the Day of the Competition:

Arrange for the following supplies to be available on the day of the competition:

_____ All materials listed above

_____ Water (both hot and cold)

_____ Measure several distances on the floor, ranging from 15 to 40 m and mark with tape. Identify each with a different letter (A, B, C, etc.) Record the lengths on an answer key.

From *Mind Builders: Multidisciplinary Challenges for Cooperative Team-building and Competition* by Paul Fleisher and Donald M. Ziegler. Westport, CT: Libraries Unlimited/Teacher Ideas Press. Copyright © 2006.

Time Out!

Time measurement is an essential part of the history of science. A number of the world's great scientists devoted at least part of their careers to measuring time accurately. Many experiments are useless unless you can measure exactly how long it takes for something to happen. This challenge will test your skill and creativity in marking time precisely.

The Challenge: Create a time delay device inside a cardboard box that will allow a marble to pass through the box in *exactly* one minute. One team member will place the marble in the box through a hole in the top. The marble must exit through a hole in one of the sides exactly one minute later.

You must use a standard size box—one used to package 10 reams of 8.5 x 11 inch copy paper and a standard marble provided to you by the coaches and judges.

Display: Investigate the history of timekeeping. Choose one important invention in the history of time measurement to research. After completing your study, design and produce a tri-fold display that describes that advance in timekeeping.

Your display must include both graphics and text.
You must use a computer in creating your display.
You must use information from at least three sources.

Performance: Create an oral presentation on the subject of time. Your presentation must last for *exactly* 1 minute. The presentation may be in the form of a skit, speech, song, or poem. Your score will be based, in part, on how close you come to the 1-minute mark. You may *not* use a watch or timer during your presentation.

Log: Your team must keep a careful written log of its research, planning, and practice. This journal must be written neatly, using a word processing program.

Your team may spend no more than $25 on this problem. All expenses must be documented in the log. Keep receipts and submit them with the documentation.

The log must also include technical drawings, drawn to scale, of the interior of your box, showing how the delay device works.

Note: If you are not certain whether a particular technique is acceptable, check with an adult sponsor *before* the day of the competition.

From *Mind Builders: Multidisciplinary Challenges for Cooperative Team-building and Competition* by Paul Fleisher and Donald M. Ziegler. Westport, CT: Libraries Unlimited/Teacher Ideas Press. Copyright © 2006.

Time Out!

Scoring Sheet

Team _____

Research Display:

    Provides details about invention and inventor(s) (max. 10 pts.) _____

    Illustrated with photos and/or drawings (max. 10 pts.) _____

    Produced with a computer (max. 5 pts.) _____

Log:

    Complete and detailed (max. 10 pts.) _____

    Includes technical drawings (max. 10 pts.) _____

    Expenses detailed (max. 10 pts.) _____

    Produced with a computer (max. 5 pts.) _____

Performance:

    Creativity: (max. 10 pts.) _____

    Strength of performance (max. 10 pts.) _____
    (Organization, stage presence, clarity)

    Meets time limitation (max. 20 pts.) _____
    (Deduct 1 point for each second over or under 1 minute)

Engineering Challenge:

    _____ Time of marble to exit box: Subtract 1.5 points for
            each second over or under 60 seconds (max. 100 pts.) _____

    Penalty points deducted _____

    Reason(s) _____

                                                                  Total [   ]

Total possible points: 200

Time Out!

Hints for Coaches

Teams must use a standard box, many of which should be available from school copy rooms, copy companies, or office supply stores. Adults running the competition should also provide several standard-sized marbles for students to work with when the problem is assigned.

There is no single "right" way to solve this problem. Possible solutions are limited only by students' imaginations. Encourage team members to brainstorm multiple ways to delay the marble in the box. They may test out prototypes of several methods, if time allows, before choosing their final design.

Possible methods to delay the marble could include a flow of sand or water, a spring-wound device, an obstruction that melts away, or a series of ramps or tracks. (Don't share these ideas with students unless they have difficulty coming up with ideas of their own.)

Once students settle on a way to design the interior of their box, they should create a prototype and test the final mechanism repeatedly to make its timing as accurate as possible.

Each team should designate one member to release the marble into the box.

Students should devise a method of timing their performances to come as close to the required 1-minute mark as possible. They should rehearse their presentation several times to test the reliability of their method and make adjustments as necessary.

Essential Supply List: marbles, copy paper boxes, stopwatches, display boards, computer access; other material requirements will vary with each team

Suggestions for possible research topics: water clock, pendulum clock, sand glass, calendars, sundial, zodiac, quartz crystal clock, cesium clock, Einstein's theory of special relativity, daylight saving time, time zones, Greenwich Mean Time, measurement of longitude. (Don't share these ideas with students unless necessary.)

From *Mind Builders: Multidisciplinary Challenges for Cooperative Team-building and Competition* by Paul Fleisher and Donald M. Ziegler. Westport, CT: Libraries Unlimited/Teacher Ideas Press. Copyright © 2006.

Administrators' Checklist

In addition to the standard Administrators' Checklist, this problem requires the following preparation:

Advanced Planning:

_____ Obtain a bag of standard-size marbles.

_____ Distribute standard marbles to coaches.

On the Day of the Competition:

Arrange for the following supplies to be available on the day of the competition:

_____ One table on which to place students' timing devices as they are tested.

_____ Extra standard marbles.

Polar Rescue

Work in the polar regions is dangerous. Storms arise with almost no warning, leaving explorers blinded in a condition called a whiteout. In a whiteout, you can see nothing—people have frozen to death 10 feet from the safety of a shelter. In a whiteout, people must find one another and find shelter with pre-planned procedures. Otherwise they are doomed.

The Challenge: Research/Display: Research the history of Arctic or Antarctic exploration. Choose a polar explorer and investigate the story of his or her quests. Then create a tri-fold display that describes that explorer's exploits. Your display must include maps, graphics, and text. You must use a computer in creating the display. Use information from at least three sources.

Oral Presentation: Retell the story of the explorer's adventure as an epic poem. The poem must be no more than 2 minutes long when performed aloud. It will be displayed for the judges at the beginning of the competition and performed for an audience during the competition.

Log: Your team must keep a careful record of its research, planning, and practice. This journal must be written neatly using a word processing program. Your team may spend no more than $25 on this problem. All expenses must be documented in the log. Submit all receipts with the log.

Rescue: To simulate a whiteout, three of the five team members will have white, five-gallon buckets placed over their heads so they cannot see. Buckets will have small holes drilled in the sides and top to facilitate hearing. The buckets will be numbered, 1, 2, and 3. The three team members will then be guided to three different locations somewhere within a half of a basketball court. Six small buckets representing data collection devices will then be placed on the court. Two targets will numbered "1," two will be numbered "2," and two will be numbered "3."

The remaining two team members are directors. They will stand at the explorers' base station—on the sideline of the court. They must guide the blinded adventurers— by voice or audible signals only—to the appropriately numbered targets. (The student wearing bucket 1 must retrieve targets with the number 1, and so on.) The three blinded students are then guided back to the base station. The task is completed when all six targets have been recovered, and all five team members are *seated* in chairs at the base station. Teams will have no more than 3 minutes to complete this task. Directors will receive alerts from the judges at the 2:00-minute, 2:30-minute, and the 2:45-minute marks.

Because this task requires students to hear guidance from their directors, **there will be severe penalties—including disqualification for a second offense—for any other team that makes distracting noise during the competition.**

Note: If you are not certain whether a particular technique is acceptable, check with an adult sponsor *before* the day of the competition.

From *Mind Builders: Multidisciplinary Challenges for Cooperative Team-building and Competition* by Paul Fleisher and Donald M. Ziegler. Westport, CT: Libraries Unlimited/Teacher Ideas Press. Copyright © 2006.

Polar Rescue

Scoring Sheet

Team _____

Research Display:

    Display includes one or more maps (max. 5 pts.)   _____

    Provides details of explorer's life and work (max. 10 pts.)   _____

    Illustrated with photos and/or drawings (max. 10 pts.)   _____

    Produced with a computer (max. 5 pts.)   _____

Log:

    Complete and detailed (max. 10 pts.)   _____

    Expenses detailed (max. 10 pts.)   _____

    Produced with a computer (max. 5 pts.)   _____

Poetry Performance:

    Quality of writing (max. 10 pts.)   _____

    Creativity (max. 10 pts.)   _____

    Strength of performance
(organization, stage presence, clarity) (max. 10 pts.)   _____

    Meets time limitation (max. 10 pts.)   _____
(Deduct 1 point for each 5 seconds over 2 minutes)

Navigation:

    _____ Targets retrieved by appropriately numbered team member
        x 5 pts. = (max. 30 pts.)   _____

    _____ Team members seated at base within 3 minutes x 5 pts. =
        (max. 25 pts.)   _____

    (Divide) ÷ <u>Time of completed rescue:</u>   _____

        Best team time to complete rescue: _____

    x 50 pts. = (max. 50pts.)   _____

    Penalty points deducted   _____

    Reason(s) _____

                                       Total

Total possible points: 200

Polar Rescue

Hints for Coaches

Prepare practice buckets for the team by drilling groups of 5 half-inch diameter holes in the sides of the buckets at approximately ear level. Also drill 10 half-inch diameter holes in the bottom of the bucket (which will be located at the top of the competitor's head when the bucket is worn). This will allow students to hear instructions from teammates and provide a little ventilation. Attach a short, doubled piece of rope to the handle of each bucket. When placing the bucket over their head, allow the handle to hang down in front of their chest. Then pass the rope under their armpits and tie it in a bow behind them, to secure the bucket over their head. Supervise students closely to prevent any choking hazard.

Teams will need to devise a system to communicate across the width of a basketball court. Their procedures will have to allow for directing three teammates, each of whom will have to be guided to two different and specific targets and then brought "home" to the base station without banging into chairs or each other.

In scoring the competition, the team that completes the rescue in the fastest time will receive the maximum points. All other team scores will be calculated proportionately, based on that score. For example, if the fastest team completes their rescue in 80 seconds, they will receive 50 points:— $(80 / 80) \times 50$. Another team that completes the rescue in 100 seconds would receive 40 points:— $(80 / 100) \times 50$.

Teams can earn partial points if they do not collect all six targets. Team members must also be seated at the sideline at the end of the 3-minute period to earn points. Teams will lose 5 points for each member not seated at the end of their allotted time.

Essential Supply List: stopwatches, display boards, computer access, three plastic 5-gallon buckets (drilled with 1/2 inch bit), lengths of rope, six small buckets, chairs, basketball court; other material requirements will vary by team

Suggested research leads: Henry Hudson, James Clark Ross, Ernest Shackleton, Robert Scott, Roald Amundsen, Fridtjof Nansen, Richard Byrd, Matthew Henson, Robert Peary, Ann Bancroft, Lynne Cox, Jerri Nielsen

Polar Rescue

Administrators' Checklist

In addition to the standard Administrators' Checklist, this problem requires the following preparation:

Advanced Planning:

_____ Obtain three clean, white plastic 5-gallon buckets. Drill five 1/2-inch holes in each side, below the handles at ear level, and 10 holes in the bottom of the bucket. With permanent marker, label with the numbers 1, 2, and 3.

_____ Obtain six small plastic buckets. With permanent marker, label two each with the numbers 1, 2, and 3.

Arrange for the following to be available on the day of the competition:

_____ Five chairs for students to sit in at the end of the rescue

_____ The large and small buckets that you have prepared

On the Day of the Competition:

_____ Line up five chairs along the sideline of the basketball court to serve as each team's start/finish point.

_____ After each team has its three members' heads covered with buckets, place the six target buckets randomly on the basketball court. Lead the three blinded team members to random locations on the court. Then start the timed competition.

The Fax Heard 'Round the World

We live in a time of amazing advances in information technology. We can store billions of words of information in home computers, communicate almost instantaneously with people around the globe, carry our computing power in small handheld devices, and teleport entire documents to distant locations. This challenge invites you to explore the digital world.

The Challenge: Each team will develop a method to demonstrate sending and duplicating a facsimile message—a simple black and white symbol or image—across the width of a basketball court, without using any verbal communication. The information must be sent digitally (1 representing black and 0 representing white), using either visual or audible signals, or both.

At the beginning of the competition, the team will be *randomly* divided into two groups—a transmitting group (two students) and a receiving group (three students.) The two groups will be positioned on opposite sides of the basketball court. A desk will be provided for each group. *Once the groups are in place, no words or other verbal signals may be exchanged between them.*

The transmitting group will then be given a digital message—a pattern of black and white pixels on an 8 x 8 square grid. Several samples are provided with this problem. Their task is to send the information to the receiving group, who will replicate and record it on a large, poster-sized grid with attachable squares. The receiving group's grid will be visible to the audience, but the sending group will not be able to see it. The entire transmission must be completed within a 2-minute period.

Research/Display: Choose an invention or innovation in digital information technology. Thoroughly research that innovation. Then, produce an attractive, informative tri-fold display that presents the team's findings. The presentation should include the following:

a. An explanation of how the technology works, with illustrations

b. Information about individuals who were responsible for the advance in technology

c. A description of the changes this innovation has produced in modern life

In addition, students must research a historical event for the following performance:

Performance: Before transmitting their message, each team will make a dramatic presentation lasting between 1 and 2 minutes, answering the question: What if _____ had had a fax machine?

In their presentation, students must imagine how history would have been different if the participants in a historical event could have communicated by fax. (For example, what if Paul Revere had a fax machine? How might the events of 1775 have been different?)

Log: The teams will submit documentation that includes:

a. Research notes

b. A script for the performance

c. A record of the team's process as it researched and experimented with solutions to the problem; a list of expenses must also be included. No more than $25 may be spent by each team. Keep receipts and submit them with the documentation.

Note: If you are not certain whether a particular technique is acceptable, check with an adult sponsor *before* the day of the competition.

The Fax Heard 'Round the World

Scoring Sheet

Team _____

Research Display:

Clearly explains how the technology works (max. 10 pts. _____

Includes details about people responsible for the innovation (max. 10 pts.) _____

Illustrated with photos and/or drawings (max. 10 pts.) _____

Log:

Detailed research notes (max. 10 pts.) _____

Includes script for performance (max. 10 pts.) _____

Expenses detailed (max. 5 pts.) _____

Produced with a computer (max. 5 pts.) _____

Performance:

Performance meets time limitation (max. 15 pts.) _____

(1 point deducted for each second over 2 minutes or under 1 minute)

Strength of performance
(organization, stage presence, clarity) (max. 15 pts.) _____

Creativity (max. 15 pts.) _____

Fax Transmission:

Meets time limitation (max. 15 pts.) _____

(1 point deducted for each second over 2 minutes)

Accuracy of transmission: (max. 64 pts.) _____

(1 point for each pixel transmitted correctly)

Bonus for a *perfect* transmission

(all 64 pixels transmitted correctly: 16 pts.) _____

Penalty points deducted _____

Reason(s) _____

Total [ ]

Total possible points: 200

From *Mind Builders: Multidisciplinary Challenges for Cooperative Team-building and Competition* by Paul Fleisher and Donald M. Ziegler. Westport, CT: Libraries Unlimited/Teacher Ideas Press. Copyright © 2006.

The Fax Heard 'Round the World

Hints for Coaches

A fax machine works by dividing a document into a grid of pixels. The pixels are then scanned in order. Each pixel is recorded digitally as either black (1) or white (0). The pixels are transmitted in order, as a series of ones and zeros. The receiver can then reproduce the document by recreating that same series of digits.

Teams will need to devise a method of sending digital information, either by using a series of visual signals (flags, flashes of light, hand signals, etc.) or audible signals (beeps, whistles, etc.) or both. They may not use any vocal signals, verbal or otherwise. They should practice sending and receiving messages written on an 8 x 8 grid.

During the competition, students will record their fax transmission on a white foam-core board marked with an 8 x 8 grid. Each cell of the grid will have a Velcro button in the center. Students will be provided with black poster board squares with Velcro fasteners attached to place in each square transmitted as black. Squares transmitted as white will be left "blank," without a black Velcro square.

Encourage teams to include some sort of verification system in their plan, so the receivers can check the message they've received or at least verify in increments that it has been received.

Teams will not know until the competition begins which students will serve as receivers and which will be senders. This is to ensure that all team members understand the entire process of sending the "fax." Make sure that each team member can perform the duties on either side of the transmission.

Judges are not likely to look with pleasure on the use of Paul Revere's ride as the subject of a team's skit. Choose some other historical event.

Essential Supply List: stopwatches, display boards, computer access, foam-core board, black magic marker, meter stick, Velcro dots (available from office supply stores), sample messages for practicing transmissions.

Other material requirements will vary with each team.

Suggestions for possible research topics: Binary number system, computers, computer programming, integrated circuits, compact discs (CDs), digital video discs (DVDs), video games, modems, digital cable, cell phones, hand-held calculators, printers, scanners. (Don't share these ideas with students unless necessary.)

From *Mind Builders: Multidisciplinary Challenges for Cooperative Team-building and Competition* by Paul Fleisher and Donald M. Ziegler. Westport, CT: Libraries Unlimited/Teacher Ideas Press. Copyright © 2006.

The Fax Heard 'Round the World

Administrators' Checklist

In addition to the standard Administrators' Checklist, this problem requires the following preparation:

Advanced Planning:

_____ Along with the problem, distribute copies of sample 8 x 8 "messages" to coaches. Reserve several of the "messages" to be used during the competition, or make several additional problems. The messages used in the competition should be of comparable difficulty (with similar numbers of black and white squares) and should be abstract shapes or designs rather than specific letters, numbers, or other symbols.

Prior to the Competition:

_____ Produce a large 8 x 8 grid (with 2-inch squares) on white foam-core board, using black marker. Mount a Velcro dot in the center of each square in the grid. Cut out about 50 2-inch squares from black poster-board, and mount the other half of a Velcro dot on the back of each square.

_____ Obtain an easel to display the grid board.

_____ Make copies of the "messages" students will be asked to transmit during the competition. Keep these hidden from the view of participants at all times.

On the Day of the Competition:

_____ Set up the easel at the receiving position on the basketball court. Arrange the easel so the foam-core recording board can be seen by spectators but cannot be seen from the sending position.

_____ Set up two chairs at the sending position. Mark the sending position with a strip of masking tape on the floor.

_____ Set up small desks or tables at the sending and receiving positions.

From Mind Builders: Multidisciplinary Challenges for Cooperative Team-building and Competition by Paul Fleisher and Donald M. Ziegler. Westport, CT: Libraries Unlimited/Teacher Ideas Press. Copyright © 2006.

The Fax Heard 'Round the World

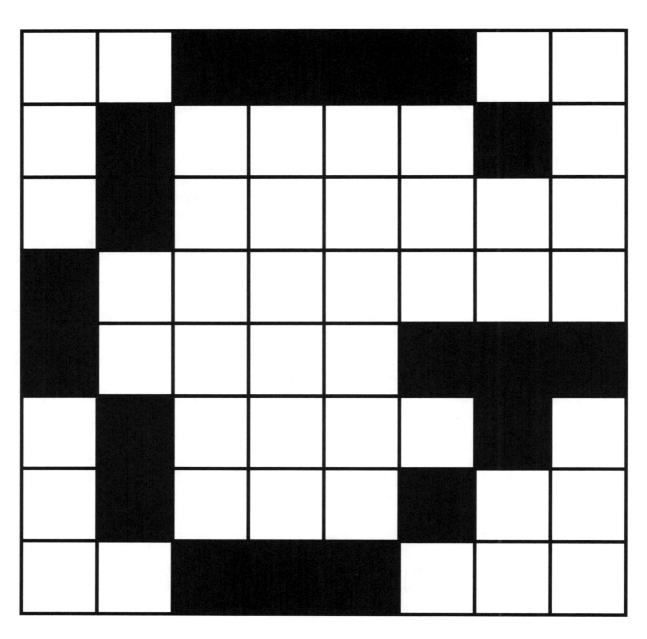

Practice Message

The Fax Heard 'Round the World

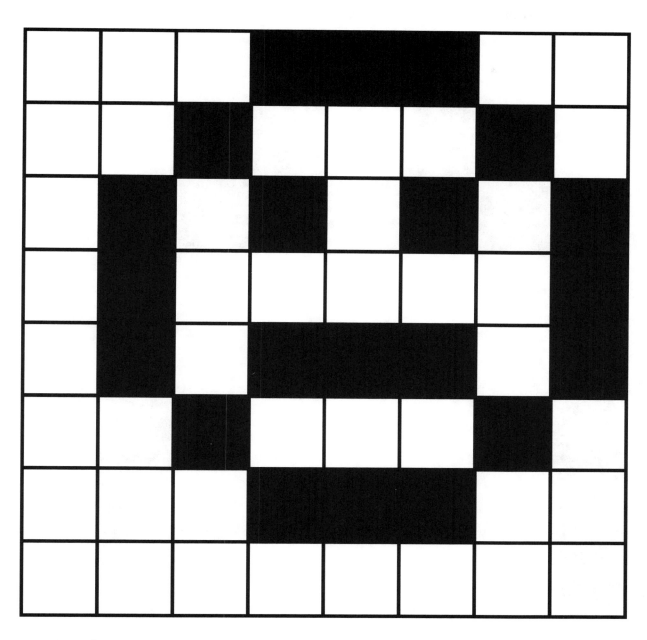

Practice Message

The Fax Heard 'Round the World

Practice Message

The Fax Heard 'Round the World

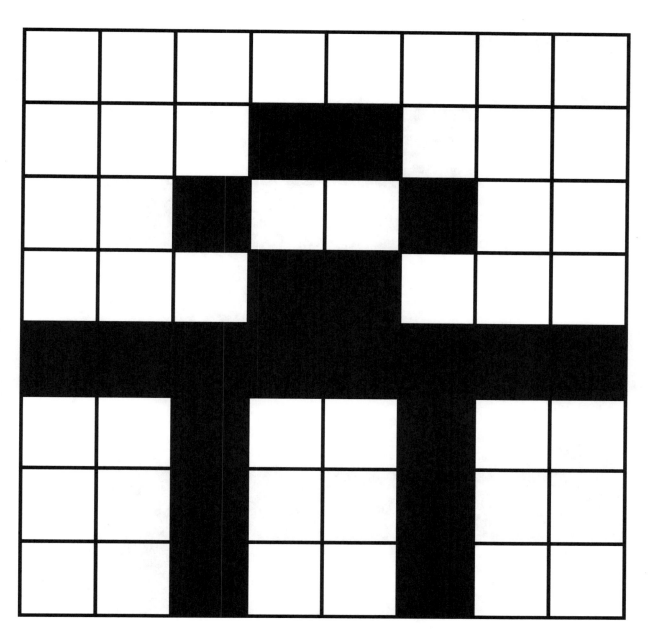

Practice Message

The Fax Heard 'Round the World

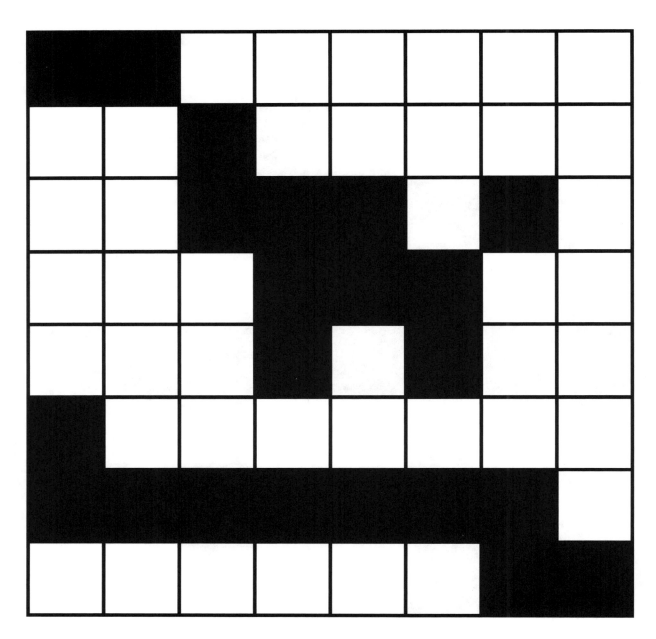

Practice Message

The Fax Heard 'Round the World

Practice Message

The Fax Heard 'Round the World

Competition Message

The Fax Heard 'Round the World

Competition Message

The Fax Heard 'Round the World

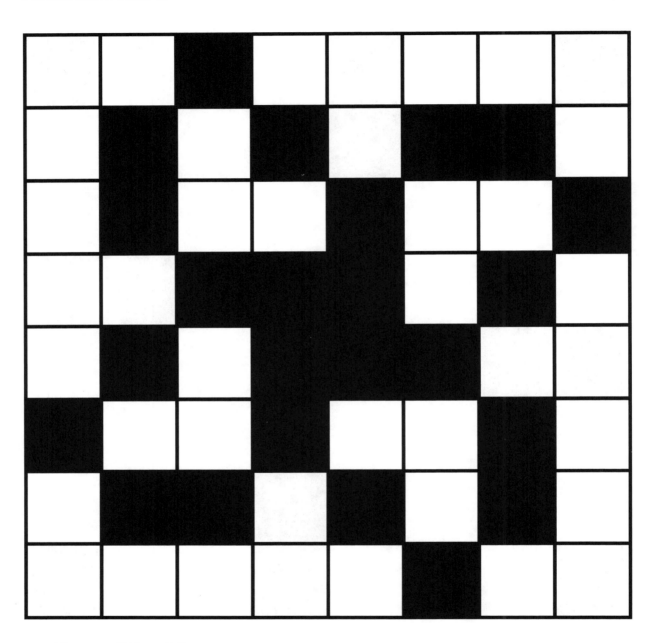

Competition Message

The Fax Heard 'Round the World

Competition Message

From *Mind Builders: Multidisciplinary Challenges for Cooperative Team-building and Competition* by Paul Fleisher and Donald M. Ziegler. Westport, CT: Libraries Unlimited/Teacher Ideas Press. Copyright © 2006.

The Fax Heard 'Round the World

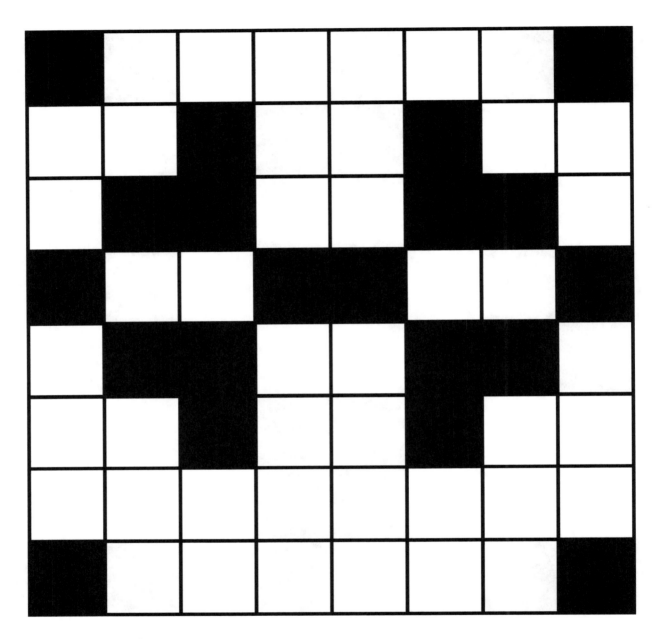

Competition Message

From *Mind Builders: Multidisciplinary Challenges for Cooperative Team-building and Competition* by Paul Fleisher and Donald M. Ziegler. Westport, CT: Libraries Unlimited/Teacher Ideas Press. Copyright © 2006.

The Fax Heard 'Round the World

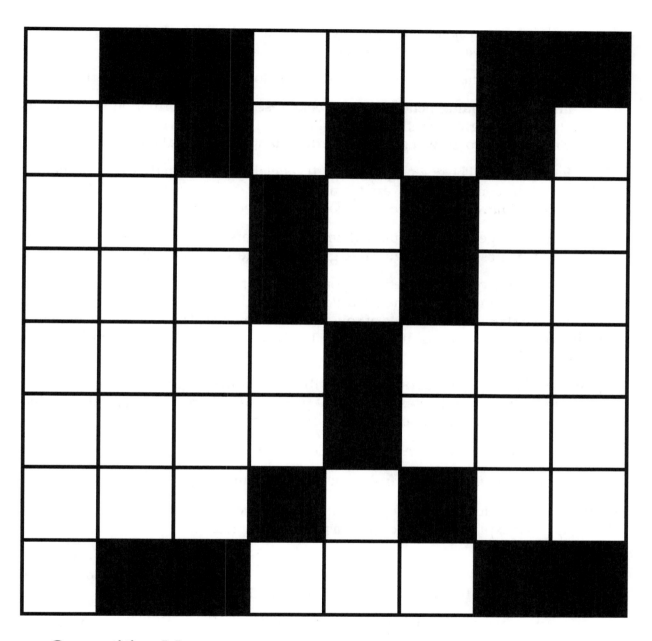

Competition Message

Green Revolution: Food for the World

The world's human population is growing, but our planet's arable land is not. People need to be fed. How do we grow more food on the limited farmland available to us?

The Challenge: Your task will be to grow the most food within a 6-week period.

First, you should spend several weeks researching information about plant growth, gardening, and methods to get the largest yield from vegetable plants. That will prepare you to grow a group of garden plants for the challenge.

Each team will be given a packet of 20 vegetable seeds exactly six weeks before the day of the competition. Every team will get the same variety of seed. However, you will not know what kind of seed you will receive until the day of distribution.

When you get the seeds, plant them in containers and care for them in the most effective way possible. Your goal is to grow the largest, strongest plants in 6 weeks.

On the day of the competition, you will present your plants, growing in their containers. You will select the 10 largest plants. Those 10 plants will be removed from the containers, rinsed free of soil, and then weighed. The heaviest set of plants will score the most points. If fewer than 10 plants survive, all surviving plants will be weighed.

Display: Research the process of plant growth. After completing your research, design and produce a poster that explains what plants need to grow, the typical plant life cycle, and what farmers and gardeners do to improve plant yields.

- Your poster must include both graphics and text.

- You must use information from at least three sources.

Performance: Your team must create a skit, interpretive dance, or musical theater production that explains the life cycle of a plant. Your presentation must last no longer than two minutes.

Log: Your team must keep a careful written log of its research, planning, and practice. This journal must be written neatly, using a word processing program.

Your team may spend no more than $25 on this problem, and all expenses must be documented in the log. Submit receipts with your log.

The log must include a script for your performance and a collection of advertisements for gardening implements and materials sold to improve crop yields.

Note: If you are not certain whether a particular technique is acceptable, check with an adult sponsor *before* the day of the competition.

From *Mind Builders: Multidisciplinary Challenges for Cooperative Team-building and Competition* by Paul Fleisher and Donald M. Ziegler. Westport, CT: Libraries Unlimited/Teacher Ideas Press. Copyright © 2006.

Green Revolution: Food for the World

Scoring Sheet

Team _____

Research Display:

    Provides accurate details about plant growth (max. 10 pts.)   _____

    Illustrated with photos and/or drawings (max. 10 pts.)   _____

    Design: attractive and carefully produced (max. 10 pts.)   _____

Log:

    Complete and detailed (max. 10 pts.)   _____

    Includes a collection of garden product information (max. 10 pts.)   _____

    Expenses detailed (max. 10 pts.)   _____

    Produced with a computer (max. 5 pts.)   _____

Performance:

    Presents clear, accurate information (max. 10 pts.)   _____

    Strength of performance
(organization, stage presence, creativity) (max. 10 pts.)   _____

    Meets time limitation
(Deduct 1 point for each second over 2 minutes) (max. 15 pts.)   _____

Plant Growth:

    Weight of plants _____ / Best team's weight _____ x 100 =

    (max. 100 pts.)   _____

    Penalty points deducted   _____

    Reason(s) _____

                                                                    Total _____

Total possible points: 200

Green Revolution: Food for the World

Hints for Coaches

A visit to a garden center, greenhouse, or nursery might be a good way to jump-start students' research.

Students will be eager to plant their seeds as soon as they get them and may also be tempted to give them *too much* care. Students should not expect all 20 seeds to germinate. Seeds may germinate more quickly if you soak them in water overnight before planting. Be alert to the following potential pitfalls:

- Make sure the seeds are planted in containers with drainage holes in the bottom. With too much water, the seeds will rot. Overwatering growing plants can be as harmful as underwatering.

- Use containers that are generous in size. Larger containers may promote plant growth.

- Overfertilizing plants can also be harmful. Too much fertilizer will kill young plants.

- Vegetable plants generally need full sun. The more sunlight, the stronger they will grow. However, beware of "cooking" them if they are growing indoors in a hot location with limited ventilation. Too much heat may kill or stunt the seedlings.

The team that grows the heaviest plants will receive a full 100 points. All other team scores are calculated proportionally. For example, suppose Team A's plants weigh 20 grams, while Team B's only weigh 15 grams. Team A would receive the full 100 points, and team B would get 15/20 of that, or 75 points.

From Mind Builders: Multidisciplinary Challenges for Cooperative Team-building and Competition by Paul Fleisher and Donald M. Ziegler. Westport, CT: Libraries Unlimited/Teacher Ideas Press. Copyright © 2006.

Green Revolution: Food for the World

Administrators' Checklist

In addition to the standard Administrators' Checklist, this problem requires the following preparation:

Advanced Planning:

_____ Purchase sufficient quantities of seed. Health food stores that sell seeds to be grown for sprouts would be a good place to shop. Make sure seeds bought at a garden or feed store are dated to be sold for the current year (some vegetable seeds are only viable for one year.) Do *not* purchase seed that has been treated with fungicide, which would expose students to toxic chemicals.

Any of the following varieties of garden seed would be appropriate for use: string beans, lima beans, soy beans, mung beans, peas, field peas, black-eyed peas, radish, sweet corn, mustard, bok choy, turnip.

_____ You may wish to conduct a germination test yourself before distributing the seeds to make sure they are viable (optional).

_____ Count seeds into groups of 20 and place in envelopes for distribution.

_____ Six weeks before the competition, distribute seed packets to each team.

Prior to the Competition:

Arrange for the following supplies to be available on the day of the competition:

_____ Plastic sheeting to protect floor from spills

_____ 5-gallon bucket of water to rinse plants

_____ Paper towels to pat plants dry before weighing

_____ A sensitive scale, preferably a digital scale. (A postage scale, triple beam balance, or electronic lab scale should all be sufficiently accurate.)

From Mind Builders: Multidisciplinary Challenges for Cooperative Team-building and Competition by Paul Fleisher and Donald M. Ziegler. Westport, CT: Libraries Unlimited/Teacher Ideas Press. Copyright © 2006.

Catapult Rescue

The people of Queezletown have been isolated by bad weather. Snow and ice, floods, sandstorms, tornadoes, plagues of locusts. Hail, sleet, and fog. Cirrus clouds!

They're running out of food. No vehicles can reach the tiny town. But wait! We can deliver the needed supplies by air. All we need is a catapult to toss food into the village.

The Challenge: Build a catapult to toss standard-sized foil wrapped chocolate balls into a target exactly 5 meters away.

Only one team member will be allowed to touch the catapult to launch each ball. You will earn bonus points by firing the catapult with some sort of trigger device.

Other team members may help prepare each shot, however. The force that propels the ball toward the target must be provided by the device itself, with no power from human muscles.

Your team will be allowed up to three practice shots first. You may choose to take fewer practice rounds if you are satisfied with your aim.

You will then have three shots to score points on the target. The closer the projectile lands to the center of the target, the more points you will score.

Display: Investigate one of the important battles in history before the year 1600. After completing your research, design and produce a bi-fold or tri-fold display that explains who the combatants were, what they were fighting about, what weapons were used, how the battle was fought, and what the final outcome was.

Your display must use both graphics and text, including a map.

You must use a computer to create your display.

You must use information from at least three sources.

Performance: Your team will write an epic poem that tells the story of your daring rescue of the starving townspeople. At the competition, you will make a presentation of that poem to the audience. The presentation must last between 1 and 2 minutes.

Your presentation may include dramatization, costumes, musical accompaniment, or other theatrical elements to enhance the audience's appreciation of your work.

Log: Your team must keep a careful written log of its research, planning, and practice. This journal must be written using a word processing program.

The log must include a copy of your epic poem.

The log must also include technical drawings of the design of your catapult.

Your team may spend no more than $25 on this problem. All expenses must be documented in the log.

Note: If you are not certain whether or not a particular technique is acceptable, check with an adult sponsor *before* the day of the competition.

From *Mind Builders: Multidisciplinary Challenges for Cooperative Team-building and Competition* by Paul Fleisher and Donald M. Ziegler. Westport, CT: Libraries Unlimited/Teacher Ideas Press. Copyright © 2006.

Catapult Rescue

Scoring Sheet

Team _____

Research Display:

Provides details about the battle (max. 20 pts.)   _____

Illustrated with maps and/or drawings (max. 10 pts.)   _____

Log:

Complete and detailed (max. 5 pts.)   _____

Includes technical drawings (max. 10 pts.)   _____

Expenses detailed (max. 10 pts.)   _____

Produced with a computer (max. 5 pts.)   _____

Includes epic poem (max. 5 pts.)   _____

Performance:

Creativity (max. 10 pts.)   _____

Strength of performance
(organization, stage presence, clarity) (max. 10 pts.)   _____

Meets time limitation (Deduct 1 point for each second over
2 minutes or under 1 minute) (max. 15 pts.)   _____

Engineering Challenge:

_____ Hits in center bull's eye x 50 pts. (max. 150 pts.)   _____

_____ Hits in outer ring x 20 pts. (max. 60 pts.)   _____

Bonus: catapult fired by releasing a trigger
(rather than released by hand) (10 pts.)   _____

Penalty points deducted   _____

Reason(s) _____

Total [   ]

Total possible points: 250

From *Mind Builders: Multidisciplinary Challenges for Cooperative Team-building and Competition* by Paul Fleisher and Donald M. Ziegler. Westport, CT: Libraries Unlimited/Teacher Ideas Press. Copyright © 2006.

Catapult Rescue

Hints for Coaches

Warn students to be **very careful** when firing their projectiles. Even chocolate can be dangerous when launched at high speeds.

Students will earn points based on where the projectile first lands, not where it rolls or bounces to a stop. They should design a catapult that fires the chocolate ball for a distance of exactly 5 meters.

Propulsive energy for the catapult must be stored in the device itself (using compression, tension or torsion with springs, twine, bending wood or metal, etc.) rather than muscle power.

Students will earn bonus points if the catapult is fired with some sort of trigger mechanism. Students who simply bend something back with their hands and then let it go will not receive that bonus.

There are a number of Internet resources students can use to investigate catapult designs.

Suggestions for possible research topics: Battles of Hastings, Agincourt, Thermopylae, Marathon, Taraori, Panipat, Aegospotami, Salimis, Actium, Ilipa, Troy, Bosworth Field, Orleans, Jericho, Siege of Jerusalem, Chaeronea, Granicus, Issus, Gaugemela, Hydaspes, Asculum, Cannae, Pharsalus, Adrianople, Tours, Lechfeld, Crecy, and many, many more.

Catapult Rescue

Administrators' Checklist

In addition to the standard Administrators' Checklist, this problem requires the following preparations:

Advanced Planning:

_____ Purchase an adequate supply of foil-covered chocolate balls.

_____ Distribute samples of the chocolate ammunition to each team along with the description of the problem.

_____ Reserve a sufficient number of chocolate balls for the competition itself.

_____ Obtain a round, shallow bowl about 30–40 cm in diameter to serve as the target's bull's eye

_____ Obtain a hula hoop to serve as the outer ring of the target.

On the Day of the Competition:

Make sure the following supplies are available:

_____ Foil-covered chocolate balls

_____ Hula hoop and target bowl

_____ Mark a firing line on the floor with tape

_____ Measure exactly 5 meters from the line. Center the target bowl there and secure it underneath with tape.

_____ Place the hula hoop on the floor so that the bowl is sitting in the center of the hoop. Secure the hoop to the floor with several strips of tape.

_____ Assign a judge to stand on either side of the target to determine where each shot lands. Teams get credit for a score even if the projectile bounces out of the target.

From *Mind Builders: Multidisciplinary Challenges for Cooperative Team-building and Competition* by Paul Fleisher and Donald M. Ziegler. Westport, CT: Libraries Unlimited/Teacher Ideas Press. Copyright © 2006.

A Tack Boat

Naval warfare in the days of sail was a great challenge. Commanders had to rely on the wind to maneuver their ships into position before they could strike against their adversaries. It was not an easy task, as you will see.

The Challenge: Construct a sailing craft armed with a pin or pins. The boat itself can be no longer than 30 cm in its longest dimension.

Using wind provided by one or two students blowing through half-inch PVC tubes—each 1 meter in length—the craft will sail across a wading pool approximately 2 meters in diameter and pop a target balloon.

The target will be an array of five balloons, each approximately 20 cm in diameter, placed side by side at water level. Popping the center balloon will result in the highest score. Popping balloons on either side of the center will also earn points.

Points will be deducted if either of the blowing tubes touches the boat.

This task must be accomplished within 1 minute.

Display: Select one particular type of sailing vessel, or an individual, famous sailing ship to research. Design and create a three-dimensional display that informs viewers about this vessel, including its construction, history, and tradition. Include one or more historical events in which this ship played an important role.

Your display must include both graphics and text.

You must use information from at least three sources.

Your team can earn up to 20 bonus points for producing a handmade model of the type of ship you have researched.

Performance: Name your sailing ship. Then write an original sea chantey that glorifies and extols the virtues of your vessel and the valiant crew that sails her.

Perform your sea chantey for the audience. Your performance must last between 1 and 2 minutes. Your team may accompany its performance by playing musical instruments.

Log: Your team must keep a careful written log of its research, planning, and practice. This journal must be written using a word processing program.

A copy of the lyrics to your sea chantey must be included in the log.

Your team may spend no more than $25 on this problem. All expenses must be documented in the log.

The log must also include technical drawings of the design of your ship.

Note: If you are not certain whether or not a particular technique is acceptable, check with an adult sponsor *before* the day of the competition.

From *Mind Builders: Multidisciplinary Challenges for Cooperative Team-building and Competition* by Paul Fleisher and Donald M. Ziegler. Westport, CT: Libraries Unlimited/Teacher Ideas Press. Copyright © 2006.

A Tack Boat

Scoring Sheet

Team _____

Research Display:

Provides details about the sailing ship (max. 10 pts.) _____

Illustrated with photos, models and/or drawings (max. 10 pts.) _____

Presented as a 3-dimensional display (max. 10 pts.) _____

Accompanied by a handmade model (bonus of up to 20 pts.) _____

Log:

Includes sea chantey lyrics (max. 10 pts.) _____

Includes technical drawings (max. 10 pts.) _____

Expenses detailed (max. 10 pts.) _____

Produced with a computer (max. 5 pts.) _____

Performance:

Creativity (max. 10 pts.) _____

Strength of performance
(organization, stage presence, clarity) (max. 10 pts.) _____

Meets time limitation (Deduct 1 point for each second over
2 minutes or under 1 minute) (max. 15 pts.) _____

Engineering Challenge:

Vessel meets size limitation (< 30 cm in longest dimension) (10 pts.) _____

Vessel floats ____ (15 pts.) and responds to wind ____ (15 pts.) _____

Center balloon popped (50 pts.) _____

_____ other balloons popped x 15 pts. (max. 60 pts.) _____

(All balloons must be popped within the 1-minute time limit.)

Penalty points deducted _____

Reason(s) _____

Total [   ]

Total possible points: 250

A Tack Boat

Hints for Coaches

Students will need a safe place to practice guiding their boat to a target. A plastic wading pool similar to the one used in the actual competition will be best. **Take care that the pool is emptied when not in use** to avoid possible accidents.

Students may not touch the boat with their hands during the competition. They should practice guiding their ships with the PVC tubes while avoiding touching the boat. Moving around the pool to blow the boat backward and make additional runs at the target is allowed.

It may be helpful for teams to identify students who have the greatest lung capacity to provide wind for the boats.

Target balloons should be inflated almost to the point of popping, so that they are more easily punctured by the boat's pin(s). Smaller balloons are recommended. Distance between notches on the balloon rack will depend on the size balloons you use. If you prefer, you could simply clamp the balloons directly onto the side of the pool.

Students may want to sharpen their boats' pins with sandpaper or emery paper. Be careful with them! Multiple pins are acceptable

Suggestions for possible research topics: carrack, cog, galleon, bark, brigantine, sloop, ketch, schooner, yawl, clipper, frigate, dhow, junk, Chesapeake skipjack, Viking longship, catamaran, caravel, corvette, or any number of famous vessels, such as the U.S.S. *Constitution*, H.M.S. *Victory*, *Challenger*, *Flying Cloud*, *Amistad*, *Mayflower*, *Godspeed*, *Susan Constant* and *Discovery*, *Nina*, *Pinta* and *Santa Maria*, etc.

From *Mind Builders: Multidisciplinary Challenges for Cooperative Team-building and Competition* by Paul Fleisher and Donald M. Ziegler. Westport, CT: Libraries Unlimited/Teacher Ideas Press. Copyright © 2006.

A Tack Boat

Administrators' Checklist

In addition to the standard Administrators' Checklist, this problem requires the following preparations:

Advanced Planning:

Obtain the following to distribute to each team with the problem:

_____ Two pieces of 1/2-inch PVC tubing, cut into 1 meter lengths

_____ A shallow plastic wading pool

_____ Produce a plywood board with five notches cut in it to mount and hold balloons in the pool.

Balloons in a plastic wading pool pond.

On the Day of the Competition:

Have the following materials and supplies available:

_____ Plastic wading pool

_____ Plastic sheeting to protect against water spillage

_____ Five-gallon plastic buckets to transport water

_____ Easily available water source (perhaps access to a spigot and garden hose)

_____ Supply of tightly inflated balloons

_____ Plywood board with five notches cut in it to mount and hold balloons

_____ Assign a volunteer to be responsible to tuck the knots of the inflated balloons behind the notches in the balloon rack, and reload them as needed.

From *Mind Builders: Multidisciplinary Challenges for Cooperative Team-building and Competition* by Paul Fleisher and Donald M. Ziegler. Westport, CT: Libraries Unlimited/Teacher Ideas Press. Copyright © 2006.

Roll Over, Beethoven

Sure, anyone can play Beethoven's Ninth Symphony *on the violin or the oboe. (Well, not really.) But can you play it on a phizzaphone, a tenor hornucopia, or a didgeridon't?*

The Challenge: Create, build and name three different, original musical instruments. Each instrument should be able to play notes of various pitches. (An unpitched percussion instrument will not meet this requirement.) Using the three instruments, your team will play a recognizable version of "Ode to Joy," from Beethoven's *Ninth Symphony*.

You will then create an original musical composition using the three instruments. You may also include and sing lyrics as part of your composition.

Each instrument will also be judged on the range of notes it can produce. A range greater than one octave will earn bonus points.

Display: Select one of the four families of musical instruments (strings, bass, woodwinds, or percussion). Research that family of instruments. Then design and produce a bi-fold or tri-fold display about the family you chose.

The display should explain the science of how the instruments produce sound and how they change their pitch and volume. It should show examples of various instruments in the family, explain where they are placed in the orchestra, and give several examples of well-known musical compositions that feature instruments in the family.

The display must include both graphics and text.

You must use a computer in creating your display.

You must use information from at least three sources.

Performance: Your original instruments will each be tested for range of pitch. Your team will then perform "Ode to Joy." Finally, you will perform your original musical composition. The composition may include lyrics as well as instrumental music. The original composition must last between 1 and 2 minutes.

Log: Your team must keep a careful written log of its research, planning, and practice. This journal must be written using a word processing program.

The log must include creative fictional histories of the three instruments you have created and technical drawings of each instrument.

Your team may spend no more than $25 on this problem, and all expenses must be documented in the log.

Note: If you are not certain whether a particular technique is acceptable, check with an adult sponsor *before* the day of the competition.

From *Mind Builders: Multidisciplinary Challenges for Cooperative Team-building and Competition* by Paul Fleisher and Donald M. Ziegler. Westport, CT: Libraries Unlimited/Teacher Ideas Press. Copyright © 2006.

Roll Over, Beethoven

Scoring Sheet

Team _____

Research Display:

Provides details about a family of instruments (max. 10 pts.) _____

Illustrated with photos and/or drawings (max. 10 pts.) _____

Neatly and attractively designed (max. 5 pts.) _____

Log:

Complete and detailed (max. 5 pts.) _____

Includes technical drawings (max. 10 pts.) _____

Includes fictional histories of original instruments (max. 20 pts.) _____

Expenses detailed (max. 10 pts.) _____

Produced with a computer (max. 5 pts.) _____

Engineering Challenge/Performance:

Instruments can play at least one octave range:

_____ Instrument 1 (25 pts. + 5 pts. bonus for range > 1 octave) _____

_____ Instrument 2 (25 pts. + 5 pts. bonus for range > 1 octave) _____

_____ Instrument 3 (25 pts. + 5 pts. bonus for range > 1 octave) _____

Successfully perform "Ode to Joy" (max. 25 pts.) _____

Original composition:

Creativity (max. 20 pts.) _____

Strength of performance
(organization, stage presence, clarity) (max. 20 pts.) _____

Meets time limitation (Deduct 1 point for each second
over 2 minutes or under 1 minute) (max. 20 pts.) _____

Penalty points deducted _____

Reason(s) _____

Total [ ]

Total possible points: 250

Roll Over, Beethoven

Hints for Coaches

When forming teams, encourage students to select at least one person per team who knows how to read and write musical notation, if possible.

Do you know how to get to Carnegie Hall? Practice, practice! The more rehearsals, the better the students' performances. Encourage students to perform boldly, in full voice.

Percussion instruments are acceptable if they can play notes of different pitches. Other unpitched percussion may also be used to accompany a team's three pitched instruments.

Most woodwinds make sound through the vibration of a reed. Students can make a simple, effective double "oboe" reed by cutting the end of a plastic soda straw in a triangular shape, and then flattening it between the teeth. Woodwinds change pitch as the length of the tube of vibrating air is changed.

The pitch of stringed instruments are modulated by changing the string's length with a finger or sliding a piece of metal or glass (like a slide guitar). Changing the tension on a string or using strings of different thicknesses also varies the pitch. Stringed instruments will sound better with some sort of resonator.

Brass instruments make sound when the player "buzzes" his or her lips into the mouthpiece. They also change pitch by changing the length of the tube or by changing the tension of the lips.

Your students may want to visit http://www.oddmusic.com/gallery/ for inspiration. They may also get ideas from listening to recordings of Spike Jones, Raymond Scott, Harry Partch, or Donald Knaack.

Topics for Research: percussion, strings, brass, woodwinds

From *Mind Builders: Multidisciplinary Challenges for Cooperative Team-building and Competition* by Paul Fleisher and Donald M. Ziegler. Westport, CT: Libraries Unlimited/Teacher Ideas Press. Copyright © 2006.

Ode to Joy

Ludwig von Beethoven
Lyrics by Henry van Dyke

Joyful, joyful, we adore Thee, God of glory, Lord of love;
Hearts unfold like flowers before Thee, opening to the sun above.
Melt the clouds of sin and sadness; drive the dark of doubt away;
Giver of immortal gladness, fill us with the light of day!

All Thy works with joy surround Thee, earth and heaven reflect Thy rays,
Stars and angels sing around Thee, center of unbroken praise.
Field and forest, vale and mountain, flowery meadow, flashing sea,
Singing bird and flowing fountain call us to rejoice in Thee.

Thou art giving and forgiving, ever blessing, ever blessed,
Wellspring of the joy of living, ocean depth of happy rest!
Thou our Father, Christ our Brother, all who live in love are Thine;
Teach us how to love each other, lift us to the joydivine.

Mortals, join the happy chorus, which the morning stars began;
Father love is reigning o'er us, brother love binds man to man.
Ever singing, march we onward, victors in the midst of strife,
Joyful music leads us Sunward in the triumph song of life.

Roll Over, Beethoven

Administrators' Checklist

In addition to the standard Administrators' Checklist, this problem requires the following preparations:

Advanced Planning:

_____ Identify contest judges with backgrounds in music. They must be able to identify the interval of an octave.

_____ Find a venue for the contest with adequate acoustical properties.

_____ Distribute copies of "Ode to Joy" sheet music along with problem.

_____ Locate and arrange for microphones and an adequate PA system to be available on the day of the competition.

On the Day of the Competition:

Arrange for the following materials and supplies to be available on the day of the competition:

_____ Electronic pitch meter (if possible)

_____ Microphones and PA system

_____ Music stands

_____ CD player and selection of classical or other music to play before and after the competition (optional).

From *Mind Builders: Multidisciplinary Challenges for Cooperative Team-building and Competition* by Paul Fleisher and Donald M. Ziegler. Westport, CT: Libraries Unlimited/Teacher Ideas Press. Copyright © 2006.

Into the Blue

Human beings have always watched the birds and wondered what it would be like to soar through the air.

The Challenge: Design and build three different paper airplanes. Each plane will be designed to perform a specific task:

1. To remain aloft for the longest possible time

2. To fly the greatest possible distance

3. To land as close to a target (10 meters away) as possible

Each airplane must be made of a single sheet of 8.5 x 11 inch plain copier paper. If you choose, you may also use one or two paper-clip weights as part of each plane.

Your team will get two trials for each of the tasks listed above. You will be scored on the better of those two attempts. Your team may use the same plane for both trials. Or you may make two copies of the identical design and use a different copy for each trial.

Airplanes will be launched from an elevated position. (The game administrator will specify exactly where the planes will be launched and inform all teams in advance.)

Display: Choose one of the pioneers of aviation and research his or her life. After completing your research, design and produce a poster that describes the important events in that person's life and his or her contributions to the history of human flight.

The poster must include both graphics and text.

You must use a computer in creating the poster.

You must use information from at least three sources.

Performance: Write a short, 2- to 3-minute script that dramatizes a central event in the life of the aviation pioneer you have researched. Prepare to perform that dramatization for the audience on the day of the competition.

Log: Your team must keep a careful written log of its research, planning, and practice. This journal must be written using a word processing program.

Your team may spend no more than $25 on this problem, and all expenses must be documented in the log.

The log must include technical drawings of your three airplanes.

The log must also include a copy of the script your team has written.

Note: If you are not certain whether a particular technique is acceptable, check with an adult sponsor *before* the day of the competition.

Into the Blue

Scoring Sheet

Team _____

Research Display:

Provides details about an aviation pioneer (max. 10 pts.)　　　　_____

Illustrated with photos and/or drawings (max. 10 pts.)　　　　_____

Clear and attractively designed (max. 10 pts.)　　　　_____

Log:

Complete and detailed; includes script (max. 5 pts.)　　　　_____

Includes technical drawings (max. 10 pts.)　　　　_____

Expenses detailed (max. 10 pts.)　　　　_____

Produced with a computer (max. 5 pts.)　　　　_____

Performance:

Creativity (max. 10 pts.)　　　　_____

Strength of performance
(organization, stage presence, clarity) (max. 10 pts.)　　　　_____

Meets time limitation (Deduct 1 point for each second
over 3 minutes or under 2 minutes) (max. 20 pts.)　　　　_____

Engineering Challenge:

Flight for distance:

÷ <u>Distance of this team's flight:</u> _____

Distance of most successful team: _____ x 50 pts. (max. 50) = _____

Flight for duration:

÷ <u>Length (in seconds) of this team's flight:</u> _____

Length of most successful team:_____ x 50 pts. (max. 50) = _____

Flight for accuracy:

÷ <u>Distance of this team's landing from target:</u> _____

Distance of most successful team: _____ x 50 pts. (max. 50) = _____

Penalty points deducted　　　　_____

Reason(s) _____

Total [　　　　　]

Total possible points: 250

Into the Blue

Hints for Coaches

Insist that students work carefully when they practice launching airplanes from an elevated position. Use a stairway or other safe location for practice launches.

Several very good books on paper airplane design are available for student reference. The three flight challenges will probably require different designs.

Students will be rewarded with better results if they fold their paper carefully and precisely. A gentle release may sometimes give better results than a hard throw.

Encourage students to experiment with different placements of the paper clips. They may be most useful in adjusting a plane's balance.

Students should make multiple copies of their designs as they prepare for the competition, in case some are damaged.

All scores are calculated in proportion to the team that has the best performance in each of the three events. For example, the team whose plane flies the farthest will receive a full 50 points. All other team scores are calculated proportionally. For example, suppose team A's plane flies 10 meters, while team B's flies 8 meters. Team A would receive the full 50 points, and team B would get 8/10 of that, or 40 points.

Suggestions for possible research topics: Louis Bleriot, George Cayley, Bessie Coleman, Eileen Collins, Glenn Curtis, Alberto Santos-Dumont, Amelia Earhardt, Robert Goddard, Samuel Langley, Otto Lillienthal, Charles Lindberg, Glenn Martin, Joseph and Etienne Montgolfier, Sally Ride, Judith Resnik, Svetlana Savitskaya, Igor Sikorsky, Valentina Tereshkova, Wilbur and Orville Wright, Werner von Braun, Jeana Yeager, Count Ferdinand von Zeppelin, and many others.

Into the Blue

Administrators' Checklist

In addition to the standard Administrators' Checklist, this problem requires the following preparations:

Advanced Planning:

_____ Identify an elevated site from which planes can be launched *safely*. This may be a set of bleachers or risers, the top of a staircase, or even a small, sturdy stepladder.

_____ Inform all team members and coaches about the selected launch site. Describe the height of the launch site and any other features that will require special planning on the part of the competitors.

On the Day of the Competition:

_____ Arrange for a metric tape measure to be available on the day of the competition.

_____ With masking tape, mark a target on the floor 10 meters from the launch site.

_____ With masking tape, mark 1-meter intervals from the launch site across the floor to facilitate measuring the distance of the longest flight.

_____ Assign judges to time the duration of the extended flight with a stopwatch and to measure the distances of the other two flights.

From *Mind Builders: Multidisciplinary Challenges for Cooperative Team-building and Competition* by Paul Fleisher and Donald M. Ziegler. Westport, CT: Libraries Unlimited/Teacher Ideas Press. Copyright © 2006.

Blowin' in the Wind

Bob Dylan said, "you don't need a weatherman to know which way the wind blows." But you do need a weathervane. And the more sensitive your weathervane is, the sooner you'll know which way the wind is blowing. While you're at it, it might as well sound pretty too.

The Challenge: Your team must create the world's most sensitive combination wind chime/wind vane. Your device will be suspended from or placed on the fold-out tray of a stepladder, exactly 10 meters from a box fan. The fan itself will be positioned on a rolling cart approximately 1 meter above floor level. The wind vane will be placed at right angles to the wind direction.

The fan, on high speed, will gradually be moved closer to the wind chime/vane. Your team will score points when your device

1. responds to the wind by correctly indicating wind direction.

2. responds to the wind by making a sound audible to the judges.

The more distant the fan is when your device responds, the more points you will earn.

Research Display: Your first task is to research climate and weather. Choose one particular weather or climatic phenomenon. After completing your research, design and produce a poster that will instruct other people about that type of event. Your poster should include information about both the causes and the effects of the event you have studied.

Your poster must include both graphics and text.

The poster must be carefully and attractively designed.

You must use information from at least three sources.

Performance: Write a folk song that tells the story of a great weather event. The song must be at least 1 minute long but no longer than two minutes. Be prepared to perform the song for the audience on the day of the competition. Your team may accompany its singing with musical instruments, if you choose.

Log: Your team must keep a careful written log of its research, planning, and practice. This journal must be written using a word processing program.

Your team may spend no more than $25 on this problem, and all expenses must be documented in the log.

The log must include technical drawings of your weather device.

The log must also include the lyrics of your folk song.

Note: If you are not certain whether a particular technique is acceptable, check with an adult sponsor *before* the day of the competition.

From *Mind Builders: Multidisciplinary Challenges for Cooperative Team-building and Competition* by Paul Fleisher and Donald M. Ziegler. Westport, CT: Libraries Unlimited/Teacher Ideas Press. Copyright © 2006.

Blowin' in the Wind

Scoring Sheet

Team _____

Research Display:

Provides details about a weather phenomenon (max. 10 pts.)   _____

Illustrated with photos and/or drawings (max. 10 pts.)   _____

Carefully and attractively designed (max. 10 pts.)   _____

Log:

Complete and detailed (max. 10 pts.)   _____

Includes technical drawings (max. 10 pts.)   _____

Expenses detailed (max. 5 pts.)   _____

Includes lyrics to folksong (max. 5 pts.)   _____

Produced with a computer (max. 5 pts.)   _____

Performance:

Creativity (max. 10 pts.)   _____

Strength of performance
(organization, stage presence, clarity) (max. 10 pts.)   _____

Meets time limitation (deduct 1 point for each second over 2
minutes or under 1 minute) (max. 15 pts.)   _____

Engineering Challenge:

Response to wind direction: ÷

Distance when this team's measures wind direction: _____

Distance when best team measures wind direction: ____ x 50 pts.
                                                                              = (max. 50) _____

Response to wind direction: ÷

Distance when this team's produces chime: _____   _____

Distance when best team produces chime: ____ x 50 pts.
                                                                              = (max. 50) _____

Penalty points deducted   _____

Reason(s) _____

Total [   ]

Total possible points: 200

From *Mind Builders: Multidisciplinary Challenges for Cooperative Team-building and Competition* by Paul Fleisher and Donald M. Ziegler. Westport, CT: Libraries Unlimited/Teacher Ideas Press. Copyright © 2006.

Blowin' in the Wind

Hints for Coaches

Electricity is dangerous. Work carefully. Use an extension cord with a ground fault circuit interrupter (obtainable at any large building supply company) in your connection to guard against any accidental shock. When you are connecting the fan to extension cords and rolling it back and forth, take care to use heavy-duty cords. Make sure not to damage the wires by rolling over them with the cart.

Scoring for the wind vane/chime sensitivity will be calculated on the basis of tenths of a meter. The team with the most sensitive device will receive a full 50 points. All other team scores are calculated proportionally. For example, suppose Team A's chime rings at a distance of 4.4 meters between fan and chime, and Team B's—the most responsive—rings at a distance of 8.8 meters. Team B would receive the full 50 points. Team A would get 4.4/8.8 or 1/2 of that, 25 points.

Suggestions for possible research topics: hurricane (general or one specific hurricane event), tornado, typhoon, thunderstorm, drought, flood, monsoon, blizzard, fog, dew, snow, hail, sleet, freezing rain, virga, cloud types, el niño, Coriolis effect, global warming, ice age, contrails, Earth's heat budget, jet stream, barometric pressure, dew point, comfort index, ocean currents

From *Mind Builders: Multidisciplinary Challenges for Cooperative Team-building and Competition* by Paul Fleisher and Donald M. Ziegler. Westport, CT: Libraries Unlimited/Teacher Ideas Press. Copyright © 2006.

Blowin' in the Wind

Administrators' Checklist

In addition to the standard Administrators' Checklist, this problem requires the following preparations:

Advanced Planning:

_____ Obtain 100 feet of extension cord, including a ground fault circuit interrupter to reduce the risk of shock.

_____ Obtain a powerful, reliable box fan.

_____ Obtain additional extension cords as needed.

_____ Make sure the location selected for the competition has still air, with no errant breezes caused by drafts, heating ducts, open windows or doors.

On the Day of the Competition:

Arrange for the following supplies to be available on the day of the competition:

_____ Rolling cart

_____ Fan and extension cords

_____ A 5- or 6-foot stepladder to suspend the wind-responding devices from

_____ Measure exactly 10 meters from stepladder. Place the fan at that location, on its cart, facing the ladder.

_____ Plug fan into extension cords, connect to outlet, and test.

_____ During the competition, remind the audience and team members to be quiet and to remain seated, so that the judges can hear the chimes and know that the wind vane is responding to the fan and not to any breeze people might create while moving about.

Paper Cranes

A flock of 25 cranes is stranded on an island. Yes, cranes can fly. But these are paper cranes. The island is about to flood, turning these lovely paper birds to pulp. They must be moved to nearby island separated from their current home by a tall fence.

Unfortunately, the cranes are also very delicate. They are made of paper, after all. They cannot be touched by human hands. Instead, the flock must be lifted from one island to the other with—you guessed it—a crane.

The Challenge: Construct a device—a crane—using at least two different simple machines, to pick up 25 paper cranes and transfer them from one "island" to another, across a fence 1 foot high. Each island will be one square foot in area, and the two islands will be positioned exactly one foot apart. The transfer must be completed within a 2-minute time period.

    The base of the crane you construct will be secured in a frame 10" x 10" (internal dimensions) built of 2" x 4" lumber. (*Note:* This challenge uses English rather than metric measures because that system remains the industry standard in the United States for the building trades.)

    The paper cranes must be transferred remotely. No team member may touch a paper bird directly, nor may the team simply scoop the cranes up. The cranes must be picked up and lifted through an arrangement of simple machines operated with pulleys and levers, for example.

    Only those cranes that are placed completely within the boundaries of the second "island" at the end of 2 minutes will be counted as rescued. Cranes that are partially within the boundaries of the island will not count.

Display: Your first task is to research simple machines. After completing your research, design and produce a display that describes and gives examples of the six simple machines. The display should also include examples of how those simple machines are incorporated into a variety of more complex machines.

    Your display must include both graphics and text.

    You must use a computer in creating your display.

    You must use information from at least three sources.

Performance: Write a series of five original haiku. Remember, a haiku is a three-line, seventeen-syllable Japanese poem. A haiku should capture and describe a natural moment, as you would with the click of a camera shutter or the opening of an eye.

    Your team will have no more than 2 minutes to recite these haiku to the audience. You may, if you choose, accompany your recitation with the playing of musical instruments.

    Your performance may last no longer than 2 minutes.

Log: Your team must keep a careful written log of its research, planning, and practice. This journal must be written neatly, using a word processing program.

    Your team may spend no more than $25 on this problem, and all expenses must be documented in the log.

    The log must also include technical drawings.

    Note: If you are not certain whether a particular technique is acceptable, check with an adult sponsor *before* the day of the competition.

Paper Cranes

Scoring Sheet

Team _____

Research Display:

Provides details about simple machines (max. 20 pts.)   _____

Illustrated with photos and/or drawings (max. 10 pts.)   _____

Produced with a computer (max. 5 pts.)   _____

Log:

Complete and detailed (max. 5 pts.)   _____

Includes technical drawings (max. 10 pts.)   _____

Expenses detailed (max. 5 pts.)   _____

Produced with a computer (max. 5 pts.)   _____

Performance:

Creativity (max. 10 pts.)   _____

Follows appropriate haiku format (max. 10 pts.)   _____

Strength of performance
(organization, stage presence, clarity) (max. 10 pts.)   _____

Meets time limitation
(deduct 1 point for each second over 2 minutes) (max. 10 pts.)   _____

Engineering Challenge:

_____ Cranes rescued within 2 minutes x 4 (max. 100 pts.)   _____

_____ Number of crushed or mangled cranes (deduct 2 pts. each)   _____

Penalty points deducted   _____

Reason(s) _____

Total [   ]

Total possible points: 200

From *Mind Builders: Multidisciplinary Challenges for Cooperative Team-building and Competition* by Paul Fleisher and Donald M. Ziegler. Westport, CT: Libraries Unlimited/Teacher Ideas Press. Copyright © 2006.

Paper Cranes

Hints for Coaches

Instructions for folding paper cranes are available on the Internet as well as in many origami books.

Cranes will be folded from paper squares no larger than 9" x 9". Gift wrapping paper makes attractive cranes.

The base of the crane that students build must fit into a 10" x 10" (internal dimensions) slot constructed of 2" x 4" lumber. (That means the slot will be 3 1/2" high.) A tight fit will help students keep the crane steady as they lift and transfer the paper cranes. Their crane may also be clamped to the 2" x 4"s. Teams that choose to use clamps must provide their own.

An example of a crane board.

Use of rope, string, hinges, pulleys, levers, and other hardware in constructing the crane is acceptable.

Folding a thousand cranes is traditionally considered a way to earn good luck in Japan. You may want to encourage students to read *Sadako and the Thousand Paper Cranes*, *Sadako* (for younger readers) by Eleanor Coerr, or *One Thousand Paper Cranes: The Story of Sadako and the Children's Peace Statue* by Takayuki Ishii.

Paper Cranes

Administrators' Checklist

In addition to the standard Administrators' Checklist, this problem requires the following preparations:

Advanced Planning:

_____ Find someone who knows how to fold origami cranes. Teach adult coaches how to fold cranes, so they can impart that information to their teams.

_____ Have students fold a large supply of paper cranes for the competition, using 8.5" x 8.5" squares of paper. If possible, use many colors of paper for aesthetic reasons. Squares of gift-wrapping paper are great for crane folding.

_____ Get a 4' x 8' sheet of plywood (or smaller, if that's more convenient). Paint two 1-foot-square "islands" with a 1-foot gap between them.

_____ Cut a 1-foot-square piece of plywood. Nail or glue it between two 1-foot pieces of 2" x 4" lumber so that it stands upright. This will serve as the barrier between the two islands.

_____ Construct a space of 2" x 4"s with an internal dimension of exactly 10' on a side. Nail or screw and glue into place, as shown in the photograph on previous page.

_____ Decorate the plywood board (optional).

On the Day of the Competition:

Arrange for the following supplies to be available on the day of the competition:

_____ A plentiful supply of prefolded paper cranes.

From *Mind Builders: Multidisciplinary Challenges for Cooperative Team-building and Competition* by Paul Fleisher and Donald M. Ziegler. Westport, CT: Libraries Unlimited/Teacher Ideas Press. Copyright © 2006.

A Question of Balance

Architects must design structures that are stable. We don't want our buildings falling over. The taller the building, the harder it is to maintain that stability, as you will discover.

The Challenge: Build a platform exactly 1 foot square. The platform must balance on a single 2" x 4" pillar of wood, at least 2 inches long. The pillar may be attached to the platform by any means you choose. However, it can rest on the floor only on the base end of the 2" x 4".

Your team will then have 2 minutes to place as many weights (1-pound bags of dried beans) as you can on the platform while maintaining its balance. The more weights you can balance on the platform, the more points you will earn. You must stop when the platform tips and loses its balance.

Your team will earn bonus points for a center balance post taller than 4". The taller the balance post, the more points you will score.

If your team has time, and chooses to make a second (or third) attempt to balance weights on the platform, they may. However, each new attempt must begin with an empty platform. At the end of 2 minutes, your score will be based on the most successful attempt.

Display: Your first task is to research great architecture. Choose one of the great structures of architectural history. Find out how it was designed and built, who was responsible for its design and construction, and why it is considered so important in the history of architecture. Or choose a particular architect. Find out about his or her contributions to the art and science of architecture. Include both buildings and techniques the architect is famous for.

After researching your subject thoroughly, create a three-dimensional display that details what you have learned.

Your display must include graphics and text. Bonus points will be awarded for including a model structure as part of your display.

You must use a computer in creating your display.

You must use information from at least three sources.

Performance: How important is balance in our lives? Create a dance, sculpture, collage, or short play that in some way illustrates the idea of balance in life. You must present your product to the audience. If your performance is a work of visual art, you will be expected to explain it orally to the judges and audience. Your performance will be limited to 2 minutes.

Log: Your team must keep a careful written log of its research, planning, and practice. This journal must be written neatly, using a word processing program.

Your team may spend no more than $25 on this problem. All expenses must be documented. The log must also include technical drawings.

Note: If you are not certain whether a particular technique is acceptable, check with an adult sponsor *before* the day of the competition.

From *Mind Builders: Multidisciplinary Challenges for Cooperative Team-building and Competition* by Paul Fleisher and Donald M. Ziegler. Westport, CT: Libraries Unlimited/Teacher Ideas Press. Copyright © 2006.

A Question of Balance

Scoring Sheet

Team _____

Research Display:

Provides details about a building or architect (max. 10 pts.)   _____

Illustrated with photos and/or drawings (max. 10 pts.)   _____

Produced with a computer (max. 5 pts.)   _____

Log:

Complete and detailed (max. 10 pts.)   _____

Includes technical drawings (max. 10 pts.)   _____

Expenses detailed (max. 10 pts.)   _____

Produced with a computer (max. 5 pts.)   _____

Performance:

Creativity (max. 15 pts.)   _____

Strength of performance
(organization, stage presence, clear and understandable)
(max. 15 pts.)   _____

Meets time limitation
(deduct 1 point for each second over 2 minutes) (max. 10 pts.)   _____

Engineering Challenge:

Number of beanbags balanced by this team _____ ÷

Highest number of beanbags balanced by any team_____ x
100 pts. (max. 100) = _____

Center post Bonus: _____ inches > 4" x 5 pts. =   _____

Penalty points deducted   _____

Reason(s) _____

Total   [   ]

Total possible points: 200

From *Mind Builders: Multidisciplinary Challenges for Cooperative Team-building and Competition* by Paul Fleisher and Donald M. Ziegler. Westport, CT: Libraries Unlimited/Teacher Ideas Press. Copyright © 2006.

A Question of Balance

Hints for Coaches

For best balance, the ends of the 2″ x 4″ pillar must be sawed very accurately and carefully. We suggest using a miter box. **Insist that students work very carefully around all sharp tools.** (*Note:* This challenge uses English rather than metric measures because that system remains the industry standard for the building trades.)

Students should make sure the 2″ x 4″ pillar is firmly connected to the platform. We recommend using both glue and screws for a tight, solid fit.

Diagonal bracing on the pillar is acceptable, but only the base of the 2″ x 4″ may contact the floor. (Do not suggest bracing to teams, but let them know it is acceptable if they think of it themselves.)

Students may want to place marks on the top of the platform as guides for the placement of weights.

The team that can balance the most weight on their platform will receive a full 100 points. All other team scores are calculated proportionally. For example, suppose Team A balances 10 pounds of beans on their platform, and Team B only balances 7 pounds. Team A would receive the full 100 points, and Team B would get 7/10 of that, or 70 points.

An example of a beanbag balancing board.

From *Mind Builders: Multidisciplinary Challenges for Cooperative Team-building and Competition* by Paul Fleisher and Donald M. Ziegler. Westport, CT: Libraries Unlimited/Teacher Ideas Press. Copyright © 2006.

Suggestions for possible research topics:

Buildings: Great Wall of China, the Parthenon, Stonehenge, Persepolis, Machu Picchu, Chartres Cathedral, Great Mosque at Mecca, Chrysler Building, Sydney Opera House, Petronas Towers, the Pantheon, Brooklyn Bridge, Angkor Wat, Golden Gate Bridge, World Trade Center Twin Towers, Guggenheim Museum NYC, Guggenheim Museum (Bilbao, Spain), Monticello, the Coliseum (Rome), Fallingwater, the Louisiana Superdome, Dulles Airport terminal

Architects: Filippo Brunelleschi, Buckminster Fuller, Antoni Gaudi, Frank Gehry, Cass Gilbert, Zaha Hadid, Philip Johnson, Louis I. Kahn, Maya Lin, Michelangelo, Robert Mills, Julia Morgan, Eero Saarinen, Kanzo Tange, Mies Van der Rohe, Paul R. Williams, Frank Lloyd Wright, Minoru Yamasaki

A Question of Balance

Administrators' Checklist

In addition to the standard Administrators' Checklist, this problem requires the following preparations:

Advanced Planning:

_____ Check to make sure you have a smooth, flat floor surface available for the competition.

_____ Obtain several dozen bags of dried beans for testing the platform. (If you prefer, you may use 200-ml juice boxes instead, which weigh about 8 oz. each. If you do, be sure to inform all teams of the change ahead of time.)

On the Day of the Competition:

Arrange for the following supplies to be available on the day of the competition:

_____ A 4' x 8' sheet of *finish grade* plywood to place on and protect the floor, if necessary.

_____ A supply of weights.

About the Authors

PAUL FLEISHER is a retired educator. He is the author of numerous nonfiction books for children as well as software and other materials for educators and worked for many years as an educator of gifted and talented children.

DONALD M. ZIEGLER retired from teaching gifted elementary students in Richmond Public Schools. He has given a presentation to the National Association of Science Teachers, and is a part time gardener, astronomer, writer, photographer, and chair caner.